The Spirit of Living Creatures

One Chosen

I0420066

James C. Lewis, M.S., Ph.D.

Dedicated To My Helpmate Marian,
A Proverbs 31 Woman,
And To Those Like Alex,
Faithful Stewards Of God's Creation

One Chosen
The Spirit of Living Creatures
Author James C. Lewis
First Edition: 2015
Available from Amazon.com, Create Space.com, and other retail outlets
Copyright © 2009 by James Lewis
ISBN—13: 978-1518708244
ISBN -- 10: 1518708242

Scriptures are from THE AMPLIFIED BIBLE, Old Testament copyright © 1965, 1987 by the Zondervan Corporation. The Amplified New Testament copyright © 1958, 1987 by The Lockman Foundation. Used by permission. In the chapter titled Winter Storm, Firstborn tries to remember the lyrics from a song sung by a mankind. The song is "A Place in the Choir." Lyrics by Bill Staines. From the album "The Whistle of the Jay". © 1998. Folk-Legacy Records, Inc.

This novel is a work of fiction. Names, characters, places, events, and incidents are either products of the author's imagination or used fictitiously. All characters are fictional, and any similarity to people living or dead is coincidental.

ENDORSEMENTS

This heart-warming story will undoubtedly captivate readers of all ages and inspire continued efforts to save North America's tallest, perhaps one of its loudest, and definitely one its most charismatic and graceful birds. – **Dr. George Archibald, CoFounder, International Crane Foundation, Baraboo, Wisconsin**

To travel through this story of God's creative work is an adventure in enlightened education. Each character whispers wisdom to the heart and mind of the reader. – **Rose Sprenger, M.Ed., retired Math Teacher, Colorado**

Jim has a tremendous way with words that makes the story of the whooping cranes' migration journey come alive. His wit and wisdom on the subject makes me think that I can't wait for my grandkids to be a little older so we can read this book together. I'm looking forward to sharing the story, as well as the spiritual applications and insights with them. Great job!! --**Kent Hummel, Lead Pastor, Good Shepherd Church, Loveland, Colorado**

"One Chosen" is an emotional tale of whooping cranes raised for and released to the wild narrated by the cranes. Divine intervention guides the birds, provides support and illustrates the unfortunate results of poor choices. Factual explanations of conservation and technical practices involved in whooping crane releases and biblical citations support the story. The emotional component typical of endangered species conservation permeates the entire adventure. "One Chosen" makes a good read for young and old. – **George F. Gee, President, Whooping Crane Conservation Association, Crawford, Maine**

PHOTO CREDITS

The Front Cover photo of cranes following Big Bird and photos on pages 18, 49, 116, and 211 were provided by Peter Clegg. The photo on page 201 was provided by Kent Clegg. The photo on page 76 was provided by Tom Stehn. Their gracious approval to use these photographs is greatly appreciated. The other photos are by the author.

ACKNOWLEDGMENTS

David Arns, Keelin Lewis, Elaine Owens, Lydia Powell, and Rose Sprenger read the entire text, at various stages of revisions, and provided valuable editorial suggestions. Members of the Christian Writer's group in Fort Collins, Colorado, reviewed parts of the manuscript and offered beneficial guidance. Their assistance is deeply appreciated. Most of all I credit my Lord and Savior Jesus Christ, and the Holy Spirit, for guiding my footsteps and directing the writing of this novel.

CONTENTS

PREFACE

**"[Even the migratory birds are punctual to their seasons.]
Yes,...the turtledove, the swallow, and the crane observe the
time of their return. But my people do not know the law of
the Lord [which the lower animals instinctively recognize in
so far as it applies to them]." (Jeremiah 8:7)**

There are fifteen species of cranes in the world, but
only two, the sandhill crane and the whooping crane, are
found in North America. The whooping crane is one of
the rarest animals in North America.[1] The United States
and Canadian governments recognize them as
Endangered, a species in danger of becoming extinct.

---

[1] The beauty of cranes is admired throughout the world.
Artistic work and statutes of cranes are seen throughout Japan,
China, Korea, and other Asian countries. Cranes are
appreciated for their qualities that humans admire. Whooping
cranes, and the other white cranes, symbolize purity. Cranes
also are a symbol of a long and fruitful life, something that man
desires. For example, some cranes have lived in captivity to an
age of sixty and seventy years and males of those ages still
fathered offspring. Cranes remain faithful to one mate for life,
also representing a union admired by man.

Only one self-sustaining wild flock of 133 birds existed in 1994. In June they nest in Wood Buffalo National Park in the Northwest Territories of Canada. In fall, they fly 2,500 miles to spend winter on the Gulf Coast of Texas. There they concentrate in a narrow coastal strip where a hurricane or disease outbreak could wipe out the entire population.

Conservationists desired to start a wild migratory flock in another location so these cranes would have a greater chance to survive. Biologists' knew it would not work to trap adult cranes and move them to a new area. Experienced adult cranes would simply fly back to their familiar home area. However, young whooping cranes learn a migration route in their first year of life while migrating south with their parents. Perhaps young cranes, raised in captivity, could be taught to follow a plane and learn a new migration route.

If such a technique were successful, these cranes would be able to start a population with new nesting and wintering sites. Then the likelihood of extinction of the whooping cranes would be greatly reduced. This story tells about the testing of such a technique and how the life of one of the research subjects was changed.

The Bible gives us examples of how, thousands of years ago, God used animals to help fulfill His purposes. You may recall the great fish that swallowed Jonah to transport him to a place near Nineveh (Jonah 1:17; 2:10). Or the donkey given the ability to see an angel and speak to Balaam his master (Numbers 22:21-33). How about lions whose mouths were closed when Daniel was thrown into their den (Daniel 6:16-23)? Then there were ravens instructed to feed the prophet Elijah each morning and evening (1 Kings 17:2-6). And what could possibly cause mother cows to abandon their nursing calves in order to return the Ark of God to Israel (1 Samuel 6:7-13)? God's personal attention even included a gourd plant and a cutworm in the life of Jonah (Jonah 4:6-7).

I don't believe most of us realize what a unique bond exists between the Creator God and those living things He spoke into being. Yes, some recognize the special relationship between God and mankind. But, many are not aware of the relationship He has with parts of His creation that man considers inferior. That relationship is the one between The Spirit of Living Creatures and other animals named by Adam. This Spirit is also known as The Spirit of Living Beings or The Spirit of Life. Some may even believe that God no longer uses lesser animals to help accomplish His purposes. So I wanted you to know Firstborn's story. He also was uniquely picked, *One Chosen*, to fulfill God's purpose on planet Earth.[2]

---

[2] The Spirit of Living Creatures, also called The Spirit of Life or The Spirit of Living Beings, is present in the wheels that Ezekiel saw in his vision of the throne of God. The Spirit of God directs all creatures, in heaven and on earth, to make them serve His purpose (*Matthew Henry's Commentary on the Whole Bible*; Ezekiel 1:21; 10:17). The Spirit of life is in Christ Jesus (Romans 8:2), the Creator, Who created all things (John 1:1-3).

THE SPIRIT OF LIVING CREATURES

CRANE NAMES

Bible names have meanings. Persons described in the Bible often behave in a manner similar to the meaning of their names or exhibit qualities their name describes. Most cranes mentioned in this book were given Bible names. Name meanings have been shortened, but their source is the book by Dr. Judson Cornwall and Dr. Stelman Smith, *The Exhaustive Dictionary of Bible Names*, Gainesville, Florida, Bridge-Logos, 2003.

PRINCIPAL FLOCK MEMBERS IN THE STORY

Ahiram (a-hi′-rum) = brother of height, exalted brother.

Firstborn = the first offspring of a mother. God said the firstborn was to be set aside to a sacred purpose and belonged to Him (Exodus 13:2). The firstborn male had authority over or responsibility for the family when the father was absent, and would receive a double share of the inheritance (Deuteronomy 21:17).

Gad (gad) = good fortune, a prophet.

Kir (kur) = a wall, a fortress.

Midian (mid′e-an) = struggle, conflict, to disagree with.

Ono (o′-no) = strength, strong, His energy.

Philetus (fe-le′-tus) = beloved, worthy of love, friendly.

Raham (ra′-ham) = merciful, love, affection.

LESS PROMINENT FLOCK MEMBERS

These are like minor actors that appear occasionally in scenes in a stage play.

Aaron (a'-ur-un) = a shining light, a mountain of strength.

Abagtha (ab-ag'-thah) = fortune, happy, prosperous.

Achor = (a'-kor) trouble, tribulation.

Deborah (deb'-o-rah) = fluent in speech.

Dorcas (dor'-cas) = gazelle, an emblem of beauty.

Izehar (iz'-har) = anointed, bright one.

Lois (lo'-is) = agreeable, desirable.

Maath (ma'-ath) = small.

Mibzar (mib'-zar) = defense, a fortress, stronghold.

Nathan (na'-than) = given of God, gift.

Nimrod (nim'-rod) = a rebel, valiant, strong, he who rules.

Pasach (pa'-sak) = a divider, separated.

Ragau (ra-gaw) = a friend.

Spook (spuk) = ghost, haunt, to make frightened.

CHAPTER 1

FIRSTBORN

"I know and am acquainted with all the birds of the mountains, and the wild animals of the field are Mine and are with Me, in My mind." (Psalm 50:11)

Three years of hard work, with lives placed in danger, would have been wasted. Gone like water twirling, twisting, disappearing down a sink drain, with nothing remaining as evidence. But, God chose otherwise. It shows how much He loves His creation. Firstborn, the one He selected to help us, was in many ways no different than others of his kind. Anyone watching him would not know he was special, unless they were aware of his heroic acts and noble character.

He was slightly taller than males of similar age. Muscles were invisible under his sleek outer covering. His graceful movements showed an inner confidence. As he walked among relatives and friends he seemed to add a sense of peace and security. It was evident they had deep respect for him, and yes, for some it was love. His white garment did seem to glisten more than others, perhaps due to the bright sun. Through the eyes of most mankind he was simply another adult of his species.

He is special in my thoughts, even though I know only parts of his story. I wonder what God saw when He chose Firstborn. Man sees and judges the outward appearance. God looks at the heart.

Join me on a beautiful October late afternoon. You know, one when the sun warms your back, and the wind is resting somewhere before its next job. Plants covering the landscape look weary from a busy growth season. Insects, sensing winter is coming, sing about their good old days. We are along the sandy shoreline in the bend of a lazy river. A flock of whooping cranes is there loafing, preening and adjusting feathers after a day's migration southward. Some wade in the shallows, bathing, occasionally finding an aquatic insect, a crayfish, or minnow to eat. My friend Firstborn is there. He is a grandfather now, walking among family and friends. Obviously, he knows much better than I what happened in that first year of his life. So I asked him if he would tell you about some of his adventures.

*****

One of the most exciting moments happened during my first winter in New Mexico. I was feeding on the edge of a harvested cornfield bordered by tall grass and weeds. The grass parted in an explosive grey-brown blur of hair, with two piercing yellow eyes, leaping towards me. The mouth looked like a wide cavern that could swallow me in one gulp. Yellow-white teeth, glistening and dripping with drool, formed fences lining each side of a tongue-laden trail leading to a dark, deep cave.

I had no time to think or aim. Instinctively, with my beak, I struck at this devilish thing coming to destroy me. I aimed for the eyes. My defensive blow was as hard as I could make it, fire-charged with a double portion of fear and hate.

The crushing force burst onto my neck and upper body, throwing me backward. Over we went, my neck twisted, his chest slamming me into the ground. The breath was forced out of my air sacs. His body continued on the same path, sliding over me, then twisting, plowing into the dirt. My head was jerked to follow, like we were attached.

I rolled to my right hoping to take flight, but I was jerked back to the left. The coyote half rose, then again lunged towards me. Thrown backward, I was unable to rise to my feet. He shook his head to the right and then left. He seemed to be tearing my head off. The rest of my body, unwilling to follow the coyote's dance, felt like a huge boulder. I could not get my legs or wings to take control. My head went wherever the coyote's head went.

He certainly was in control. Wherever he went, I had to follow.

The air filled with dust and dirt from our thrashing about. Everything looked hazy. I gasped for a breath of air. I couldn't seem to open my beak. Over and over we both rolled. Growling, he first jerked his head away, then pushed back towards me. Every move he made forced my body to respond. I was helpless. He outweighed me. His quick movements kept me off balance. Any moment I thought he would finish me off. His jerking about continued. I ached all over. I hurt so badly I could not tell where his vicious jaw gripped me. Every muscle seemed to be ripped from me. The twisting and turning continued forever.

Finally he seemed to be tiring. Tearing leaps and twisting turned to shorter jerks, tremors, shaking, and whining. I felt like I was strangling. This must be it. What a disappointing end to my life. Who will lead the flock when I am gone? I had so hoped to be able to migrate back north to the ranch in spring. I was too exhausted to struggle any longer. Perhaps I was dreaming, unable to fully awaken, drifting in and out of consciousness. I wanted to go to sleep, to end this terrifying battle.

Suddenly he was still. The choking dust began to settle. His head was next to mine. I gasped for air. His eyes were wide open, staring towards me. Was he about to lunge at me again? I breathed deeply, trying to regain strength. I heard voices, distant at first, then closer.

"Firstborn? Firstborn?"

I tried to answer but was too weak, unable to open my beak.

"Firstborn, can you hear me?"

It was Ono's voice. Perhaps he had come to help me fight the coyote. I pushed up with my right wing and tried to get my legs beneath me.

"He's moving. He's not dead!" Ono said.

I thought Ono was warning me that the coyote was moving. Later, I learned he was telling some of my friends that I was alive.

My immediate thought was that the coyote must be getting ready to finish me off. I struggled to get up. Perhaps I could use the last of my strength to protect Ono. I tried to pull away from the coyote, but my beak seemed captured by his head.

Suddenly my beak broke free and I staggered backward. Dimly I could see several of my friends coming towards me. This time I was able to shout a warning. "Watch out, he's still moving!" They stopped.

Spreading my wings in a threat posture, I prepared to strike before he attacked. He did not move. I tried to clear dust from my eyes. He was motionless, lying on one side, eyes wide open, head stretched forward between his paws. His forehead was dark with blood.

The end of my bill was bloody and near my face it throbbed with pain. I must have injured it in the fight. Still the coyote was not moving. Was he unconscious? I should escape before he wakes up.

Figure 1. Ono, one of Firstborn's companions, still has juvenile feathers on his head and neck. Whooping cranes use their large thick bill for probing in the ground and capturing food items.

"Firstborn, are you okay?" Ono asked.

I hurt all over. Of course I was not okay. My right shoulder muscles did not follow my commands. The right wing drooped and did not fold beside my body. My legs were so weak they were shaking. I sat back on my hocks. "Stay back, Ono, he may be ready to attack again."

"He's been still quite awhile, Firstborn. We watched you lying there for a long time before we became brave enough to get closer. I think he's dead. Peck him. See if he will move or wake up," replied Ono.

Ono wants me to get close enough to peck the coyote? He must be crazy! Does he think I am?

I just tore loose from that beast! Now Ono expects me to attack it? I imagine it's pretending to be knocked out, ready to grab me again!

Huh. He hasn't moved. How odd! Did I knock him out?

"Firstborn, oh, I'm so happy you are okay. You were so brave to attack the coyote," said Raham.

I attacked him? I must have been out of my mind or half asleep! If I make a mistake like that again, I won't live to tell it. ... Yet, he is still. The hole near his eye must be where I struck him.

Kir boldly moved behind the quiet coyote, jabbed a hind leg, and jumped back. "You got him alright. He's not feeling anything now," said Kir.

"This battle will go down in crane history. Wow, I think it's the first time a crane ever won a fight with a coyote," replied Ono.

"Look, he struck him beside his eye. See the hole where Firstborn's beak hit him!" said Kir.

"There's a mankind watching us from the side of the field. We better move farther away," said Gad.

"Firstborn, can you walk?" asked Raham.

"I think so, Raham." I rose slowly. All my parts seemed to work, but with difficulty. Limping, one wing hanging in an awkward position, I slowly moved across the field with my companions.

After we were some distance away, the mankind walked out to the coyote's body. He examined it, grabbed one foot, and dragged its body across the field to a truck. The remainder of the day was a blur. They were telling me how brave I was. I was hurting too much to argue. I slept most of the time, trusting others to remain alert for danger.

In late afternoon, I drank from a rain puddle and swallowed a few grasshoppers. It revived me enough to answered my brain's instructions this time. At our roost[3], even some of the sandhill cranes were talking about the fight they saw between a coyote and me. It began to

---

[3] A roost is where cranes spend the night. They usually fly there about dusk and land on the ground along a lake, river, or marshland. As darkness approaches they walk out into the shallow water until they are far enough from the shoreline to feel safe from coyotes and bobcats. They do not roost in trees like many other birds.

sound like I was a living legend. Bruises and sore muscles kept me from sleeping soundly that night.

Next morning I was hungry enough to limber up my joints and fly to a field to feed. However, weeks passed before I fully recovered from wrestling with the coyote. I did not go hunting for him despite what you might have heard in stories others told about me.

I know it must be difficult for you to understand how I happened to be in New Mexico. You may also be wondering, who are Gad, Ono, Raham, and Kir? It will make more sense if I start my story at the beginning.

CHAPTER 2

MY NEW WORLD

Mom greeted me when I tumbled free from my egg. Most cranes also have a father to help raise them. I'm not complaining when I tell you I only had a mother. I never met my father. Well, yes, I suppose it is sad that I never knew my father. But, at first I did not realize I was supposed to have a father. How can you feel something is missing when you don't know it's supposed to be there? I also was not raised like most young cranes that have only one brother or sister. I had a bunch of brothers and sisters. Come to think of it, I really was fortunate.

And Mom, well, later on I found out she was quite different. I mean she was not at all like most crane mothers. If she was so different, what made me think that she was my Mom? That's not a tough question. Somehow I just knew she was Mom. I mean, didn't you know your Mom's voice? She had been calling to me, encouraging me to come out, while I was still inside the egg. I had trouble focusing my eyes when I first broke free and rolled out. Still, I could see the hazy, big, tall thing that sounded like Mom.

She did all the things I thought a Mom is supposed to do. When I first became hungry she offered me a snack, something small, white, and wiggly. I pecked at it and got a moist something on my tongue. A few more pecks, and with gusto, I swallowed my first mealy worm. Soon, she was feeding me moist tadpoles and earthworms. Except for eating, of course, our walks following Mom were my favorite time.

Every day she led us, her family, to fields filled with grass, flowers, bugs, and other interesting things. We were growing fast and rather clumsy. Sometimes our feet became tangled in grass blades or other plant parts. Our tumbles provided lots of laughs. The oldest chicks, by a few hours or several days, were first in the line following Mom. Trailing behind were the young, smaller chicks. With their wobbly legs they found it hard to keep up with us older chicks. But we all became stronger as the days passed. Then Mom moved faster and our walks lasted longer.

Mom would flap her long wings up and down. I would copy her flapping with my little short wings. It was good exercise. Often she would stop to let us rest and play. It was fun to chase grasshoppers, butterflies, or leaf hoppers. I would pick at leaves and move them about. That is how I first found a cricket and discovered they were good to eat. She would lead us until the youngest chicks became tired.[4]

I was growing fast and needed lots of food. Mom fed me some large earthworms. They were great and filled my stomach. Soon we all learned where to find worms after it rained or when the mankind watered a field. We had our own fast-food walk-through. The first to find a worm was the first one served. Life was good.

I had no doubt that Mom was *my Mom,* until I was several weeks old. One morning, she led us to a field to feed on bugs and worms. Soon I was so full I could hardly walk. So, I squatted in the shade from tall grass to watch others searching for worms. Mom left us alone while she went somewhere to take care of other business. A red-winged blackbird perched on a bush near me.

"Why do you follow a mankind?" asked the blackbird.

"What are you talking about?" I answered.

"I have seen you and your friends following a man since you were small. Why aren't you afraid of him?"

"We don't follow a man. We follow our mother!" I replied.

---

[4] Imprinting is a type of learning that occurs early in the development of ducks, geese, cranes, and some other birds. Crane chicks instinctively follow their parents within a few hours after hatching. They will follow a substitute parent, such as a human, that is present when they hatch.

"You are little cranes. I have seen your kind before in the marsh by the river. I know what mother cranes look like. You are not following one. You are following a man! They are dangerous! They shoot some of us birds!" the blackbird answered.

"I don't believe you. Stop talking that way about my mother. She loves, protects, and feeds us. We don't need to be afraid of her."

"Suit yourself. This man may be nicer than some, but I don't trust him. Here he comes again! I'm leaving."

I looked up. Sure enough, I could see Mom coming towards us. Can you imagine, how silly of the blackbird, calling Mom a mankind? Hmph! You can't trust a blackbird. I imagine he tells lies to upset and worry other birds. But a chill ran up my backbone. And my stomach was bothering me. I had trouble thinking clearly. The first seeds of doubt, of questioning, had been planted in my mind.

A few nights later, I was sleeping lightly when an owl called softly.

"Matilda."

"What do you want?" I asked, still half asleep.

"I'm not talking to you. Is your name Matilda?" said the owl.

"No. Why did you wake me?"

"You woke yourself up. The other chicks are still asleep."

"Then who were you talking to?" I replied.

"I was calling my mate over yonder in the woods."

"If your mate is over there, what are you doing in the tree by my home?"

"I like to eat on a regular basis. Lots of mice live in the meadow by your pen. At night they run over and eat scraps you chicks leave where you are fed. I thought I might catch one of those plump mice. But they won't come around here with you jabbering away," grumbled the owl.

"What's a pen?"

"It's the fenced area the man puts you in at night. He is smart enough to do it so coyotes and I can't eat you," the owl chuckled. He seemed to find my question funny and the answer obvious.

"Why would anyone want to eat us? Worms are much better!" I replied confidently.

"Eat what you like. I'll take a young crane burger over worms any day," replied the owl with a hungry glance at my sleeping companions.

"What do you mean a man puts us in the pen?" I asked.

"The mankind who's always raising some kind of birds around here, pheasants, quail, partridge, and now you cranes. Trouble is he's so careful, and protects his birds. He acts like a mother hen."

"Would you eat my Mom?" I asked with a tremble in my voice.

"Never have seen your mother, but I have seen mother sandhill cranes down by the river. Sometimes I snooze there in cottonwood trees during daylight. Mother cranes are rather big for me to tackle. Nope, I have never seen a mother crane around here. But, a mankind acts like he's your mother."

"A mankind acts like my mother? What do you mean," I asked.

"Yes, as silly as it seems. A man acts like your mother. Anyway, I'm leaving. No smart mouse will come around here with you talking."

So, the great horned owl flew across the meadow to join his wife in the woods. Owls are supposed to be wise. He said he never saw a mother crane around here, only a man who acted like a mother crane. Mom was with us in plain sight every day. A blackbird also said my mother was a mankind. I was confused. If the one we called

Mom was not our mother, who was she? Where was my Mom? Soon I fell into a troubled sleep.

At daybreak, when my brothers and sisters woke, I said nothing about the owl. I wondered, is Mom my mother? I watched closely when she came to put food in our feeding tray. Well, to be honest, she didn't look much like us. What looked like a bill had two small holes in the bottom. It looked like food in the bill would fall out those holes. I never saw her bill open. There was another place, below her bill, that opened and closed when she made noises. And there was always something on her head with a shelf that stuck out over her eyes, shading her forehead. We chicks didn't have such a shelf. I expected we would grow one later so we would be like Mom.

Her eyes were in the front of her head, unlike ours on each side of our head. Her wings were like long poles, not flat like ours. If she had feathers, they were covered by some loose-fitting material. She had long legs, but walked different than us. When she stepped forward, the middle of the leg pointed where she was going. Our legs did the opposite, bending and pointing where we had been. I could not see three toes in front of her feet, only a rounded hump. Was it possible she was not my mother? Was she a mankind, a human?

Until then, I was eager to follow close behind Mom when we went for walks. That day, however, I felt uncomfortable being close to her. I stayed at the rear of the flock. The time in the field was not as much fun as usual. I didn't play with my brothers and sisters.

Raham noticed the change. "Firstborn, do you feel ill? You don't seem as lively as usual."

"Oh, I was thinking about something. I feel okay."

Raham didn't look convinced. Still, I was not ready to explain further. There wasn't much chance to be alone, to think more about what the owl said, until nighttime. I thought I knew the answer to my question, but it was not comforting.

I suppose I should introduce Raham because she and I are good friends. She was the first chick I met, no pun intended. She always was a friend, but our first meeting did not seem to go so well. I had only been out of the egg long enough for my down feathering to dry. I walked over to another recently hatched chick. Hi, what's your name?"

"Raham. What's your name?"

"Firstborn, at least it sounded like that when Mom called me."

"Your name sounds rather important. What does it mean?" she asked.

"I'm not sure. I guess it means I was the first one to hatch," I replied.

"How long have you been out?" she responded.

"Not too long. And you?"

"About as long as you. When I first looked around you were already out," Raham answered.

"We seem to be the speedy ones." I was proud I hatched before the others.

Raham did not reply. Looking first at her toes, and turning her head to study a feather that appeared slightly out of place, she began preening. She seemed unsure she wanted to be known as being "speedy".

Somehow our first meeting did not go well. It left me feeling uncomfortable. I stood there, unable to think of anything to say, feeling awkward, silent, as I watched another chick break free from an egg. "Well it has been nice meeting you. I believe I'll walk around and say hello to some other new arrivals," I said.

But, after what I thought was a failed attempt to make friendly conversation with her, I didn't feel like talking with anyone else. So I moved to a distant edge of the pen and stood alone. My first meeting with Raham was not too exciting. Later, things improved in a way I had not expected.

One reason for the improvement was Midian, who was bigger and heavier than most of us chicks. He walked with a swagger and seemed to like to be bossy. When Mom put out food for us he would push others away and eat more than his share. One day, Midian started chasing Raham.

"Leave me alone, you big bully," said Raham.

"You know you like to be chased," replied Midian.

"Not by goons like you," said Raham as she continued to run.

"If I'm a goon, you are a goner." Midian tipped his head back ready to peck her.

As they ran by, I gave him a sharp peck on his head.

"Ow!" Midian looked surprised, stopped running, and rubbed his head with a wingtip. "This is no business of yours. Are you looking for trouble?"

"I make it my business when you pick on my friends. If you behave you won't find trouble."

"Don't ever make the mistake of pecking me again," Midian said. Then he walked away.

I ignored him and continued to straighten my feathers.[5]

---

[5] Downy feathers of whooping crane chicks are a cinnamon brown color. At about 50 days of age, new feathers are reddish cinnamon on the head and neck, and cinnamon brown with some white on the body. Male and female whooping cranes are similar in appearance.

Later I came up behind Raham as she picked petals from a flower. She said "He loves me," as she removed one petal, and "He loves me not," as she picked the next petal, and so on.

"What kind of game is that?" I asked.

She seemed surprised, and looked embarrassed. It was obvious she had not heard me approach.

"Oh, it's simply a way of passing time when a flower has lots of petals," she said as her cheeks turned pinkish.

I did not realize how much my pecking of Midian influenced what Raham thought about me. Our friendship improved from that day forward.

CHAPTER 3

THE SPIRIT

For many are called (invited and summoned), but few *are* chosen." (Matthew 22:14).

Mom kept us in a large, fenced area with a small stream running through it. The fence and overhead netting protected us from foxes, hawks, or anything that would eat us. By then the entire flock had learned to stand (roost) in water at night. I stood near friends who, unlike me, were quickly sound asleep. My mind was still wrestling with the troubling question about Mom. Could she be a mankind? I finally dozed off long after the others were asleep.

Sometime during the night I was startled by a bright light and a voice 'Firstborn!' It was painfully loud, like the sound of many waterfalls, or a thunder clap. It hurt my ears. To my surprise, none of my friends woke up. The light was so bright I could not see who or what was there. Trembling, I crouched down, legs so weak I thought I would fall over. I tried to find somewhere to hide, expecting any instant to be hit by something. My stomach suddenly felt too full to hold those tadpoles I ate a few hours earlier.

"Fear not, Firstborn, leader of the flock, gallant warrior, grandfather of many cranes. I have a job for you."

"I-I-I-I'm,-I'm sorry, whoever you are. You are mistaken. You have the wrong crane. I am not yet fully grown. I do not lead others. I am too young to be a warrior or a grandfather. If you will dim the light a little, I may be able to see you."

"I am The Spirit of Living Creatures. My light cannot be dimmed. It pierces all darkness. Firstborn, I see you as you are now and as you will be in the future. Even in the days of youth you can be a gallant warrior. Your kind is in danger of becoming extinct, of no longer existing on planet Earth. You are a whooping crane. Fewer than 200 of your kind are alive in the wild. Some men are trying to save your species from becoming extinct. I have chosen you to help.

"You are troubled, wondering if the one you call 'Mom' is your mother. Actually, 'Mom' is a mankind. Some other humans collected eggs from whooping cranes that live in pens. The eggs were delivered to the mankind you call 'Mom,' he hatched the eggs. Your brothers and sisters came from more than a dozen mother whooping cranes.[6]

"I am going to give you special abilities and spiritual gifts. You will need them to complete the job I have for you. I want you to help the mankind form your crane friends into a Team to follow him and migrate south this fall. Use the wisdom and abilities I give you to lead your friends. In winter, you and your companions will have to learn how to survive in the wild. Next spring you must find your way back north without the assistance of men.

"I will be with you whenever there is special danger. I chose you like I have chosen other animals in the past. You will understand the language of man. I once gave that gift to a donkey belonging to a man named Balaam.

"In your innermost being you will know My Truth found in the Bible. I give you Wisdom to know other things your friends do not know. You will be changed when this glowing coal, from My altar, touches your beak."

---

[6] The name of the whooping crane likely came from their loud Unison Call that can be heard up to a mile away. This call can be a duet by a pair of cranes in a mating display or a threat to other cranes. The windpipe of an adult crane coils in the breastbone and is almost five feet long. This length is one reason their calls can be heard from a great distance. Whooping cranes are the tallest birds in North America. An adult male can be four and a half feet tall. That is five to eight inches taller than the tallest sandhill cranes.

Something glowing red came out of the blinding light and touched the tip of my bill. That's all I can remember about that night. I overslept the next morning. As you know, that is unusual for us birds.

Raham gently woke me. "Firstborn, you seemed so tired. I hated to wake you. But, mother already fed us, and the others have eaten. Soon, she will be back to lead us into the fields. I thought you would want to eat something before she returns."

I looked at her without moving my head and neck from where it was tucked among feathers along my side. "Yes, I am tired, actually exhausted! Thank you for waking me." I slowly raised my head and turned to face her.

"You look different! Your face seems to be shining. The tip of your bill looks red. Do you feel okay?" asked Raham.

"I guess, ah, maybe I was in too much sun yesterday," I said as I suddenly remembered that glowing coal coming towards my beak. "Well, -- oh, -- ah, I feel fine. In fact, I feel great. I'm so hungry I could eat a mouse or baby blackbird."

"What a terrible thing to say. Why would anyone want to eat a yucky mouse?" Raham exclaimed.

"What's wrong with that? We cranes do eat such things at times," I said.

"Whatever gave you such a crazy idea?" she replied.

Actually, I surprised myself when I said we cranes ate mice and baby birds. Where did that thought come from? The Spirit that visited me last night -- or was it a dream -- said I would know about things my friends did not know. Was the idea about eating mice, or a baby bird, one of those? Or, was my imagination going wild? Raham would surely think I was crazy if I told her what happened last night, about the vision, or dream, whatever it was. I needed to end our conversation.

"I'd better go eat some of the breakfast Mom brought us or she will be here to lead us to the fields before I can get any." I quickly headed for the feeding trough to avoid more questions.

What happened to me? Normally, I faithfully awoke at daybreak to worship the Creator Who made me, the One Who daily provides me with food and all my needs. Offering Him songs and words of praise seemed to be the natural thing to do. Even the mankind's Bible says that birds should "Praise the Lord from the earth, ... Beasts and all cattle, creeping things and flying birds! ... Let them praise and exalt the name of the Lord, ..." (Psalm 148:7, 10, 13).

I wondered why a command from something called the Bible flashed into my mind. What is a Bible? Instantaneously I knew the Bible is a book of God's instructions, a love letter, to His mankind children, telling them how to be happy and to have an abundant life. Again, I remembered the Spirit said I would have an inner knowing about things I had not experienced. Wow! And double Wow!

I decided I would try to act as normal as possible and take part in this day's routine. But how could I act normal when I had been visited by The Spirit of Living Creatures?

Following Mom gave me special pleasure that morning. I knew something none of my friends knew. Mom was a human, a mankind. Still, I wasn't ready to tell my friends that she was a mankind. I didn't think they would believe me. I needed more time to think about what happened, and the visitor last night.

Something called The Spirit of Living Creatures visited me. He told me to lead my companions to migrate south in fall. I wondered, what does it mean to migrate? As soon as I thought of that question, I somehow knew the answer. To migrate means to fly from one place to another at certain seasons each year. Birds that spend summer in the north usually fly south in the fall. They spend winter in places where it is warm and food is easier to find. In spring, they return back north to nest and raise their young.

"Wow, that's amazing," I said to myself, surprised that I suddenly received the answer. But, I didn't realize that I spoke loud enough for anyone to hear me.

Raham walked over when she heard me. "What's amazing?" she asked.

"Oh, uh, something I was surprised at thinking."

At that moment I heard loud laughter and excited talking of friends. I wouldn't have to explain what had amazed me if I drew our attention to the activity of our friends.

"Come on, Raham, let's go see what's going on." We walked over to see what had excited our friends.

"Ha, ha, ha," Ragau was still laughing.

"What's so funny?" asked Raham.

"Ono was searching for crickets," answered Ragau. "He found a little grassy nest with six tiny, baby mice in it, almost hairless. Their eyes were not open. Without hesitating, he ate three of them like they were June beetles. Aaron showed up at that moment. He quickly ate the others. They were surprised that eating them seemed so natural. They said they were tasty. It seemed funny, like crazy, to the rest of us, so we all started laughing."

"Oh," said Raham, looking like the thought upset her stomach. Suddenly the look on her face changed. She frowned, seemed puzzled, gave me a questioning look, but said nothing, keeping her thoughts to herself.

Perhaps she remembered our earlier conversation when I said whooping cranes eat mice and baby birds.

"Brrrraaaaaaak," belched Aaron.

"Gross," said Nathan, laughing. "Don't you have any manners?"

"More than I do," said Ono. "Baaarrrrraaaaakkkk-ccccckwwwzzzhug, these mice bring out the best in us."

Then another disturbance attracted my attention. Achor was chasing Spook. Sometimes big chicks like Achor or Midian were mean. They would bully, chase, and peck the smaller chicks. I didn't think it was fun or nice. They especially seemed to enjoy pecking Spook, the smallest and youngest of our flock. Someone nicknamed him Spook because he was so nervous. He was jumpy, easily frightened by sharp, loud noises. Mom also didn't like us pecking each other. Whenever she was around she would separate the ones doing it.

I ran as fast as possible and bumped into Achor, knocking him to the ground.

"Oh, excuse me, Achor," I said in a tone of voice that let him know our collision was not an accident.

Achor gave me a dirty look, but said nothing as he got up and walked back in the direction from which he came.

Later, Mom left us alone to feed and loaf in an alfalfa field. The sun was warm on my back. My stomach was full of leaf hoppers, a lady bug, two grubs, and three worms. Life was good. The sun made me drowsy. Some of the flock dozed in the sun. Others continued to chase grasshoppers or crickets. I had closed my eyes for a moment when I heard a cry of alarm, pain, and anguish that pierced my innermost being. Instantly I crouched low on the ground fearing a blow from something. When I looked up, a shadow passed over me.

A golden eagle flew between me and the sun. Hanging between the eagle's talons, his head and neck dangling below his body, was Nathan, one of the youngest in our flock. The eagle, carrying the reward of its attack, turned toward the forest atop the mountain. There, most likely, his hungry, impatient young waited in a nest.

I was unable to stop shaking. My legs felt like limp noodles. It seemed every bit of strength had drained from my body. I had no control. I crouched among alfalfa clumps, motionless, trying to look invisible. Such a beautiful day had turned tragic in a matter of seconds. I searched the sky, fearing there might be other eagles, but could not see any.

Slightly raising my head, I had difficulty seeing my friends cowering beneath clumps of grass or anything offering an emergency hiding place. They also appeared terrified, as though expecting another attack. Then Mom came running, calling to us. Evidently, she had seen the eagle attack. We ran to her, knowing she would protect us. She led us into the pen and closed the door. Inside I felt safe.

Only then did I fully realize what had happened. Death crushed joy and innocence from our inexperienced little flock. A friend was violently taken from us. I had tasted fear mixed with anger, bitter, deep within my stomach, anger at the thief who stole life. It was not fair. Nathan did nothing to deserve the eagle's attack. His name meant "gift, given of God." He always seemed happy, pleasant, a good companion. I felt guilty for being thankful the eagle did not get me. And also because I could name one or two others I wished the eagle had taken instead of Nathan. Grief draped over us like a soggy, wet fog. There was no laughter or energy for play.

At dusk, I roosted in the stream, standing in water up to my hocks. My mind was in turmoil despite listening to the peaceful sound of water flowing over fine rock, beside grass blades. I believe everyone had difficulty sleeping. Some were crying out as though having troubled dreams.

The next day began with a new experience that helped take our mind off Nathan's tragedy.

"Here is Mom again with the square box that sits on round things," said Ono.

For the past few days she had parked it awhile near our pen with something called an engine making noise. I guess she was trying to get us used to it. Later I learned it was a Polaris Explorer All Terrain Vehicle, sometimes called an ATV.

However, on this particular day Mom left it right next to our pen door with the engine running. Then she opened the door to call us for our morning exercise. Carefully, slowly, I left the safety of my home, out the door, racing away from this loud, vibrating monster. Mom sat on it, slowly moving away, while calling us to follow. I timidly followed, frightened by the size and sound of this thing. She led us to a field to feed, then left the box there while she went elsewhere.

Several hours later she returned, started the engine, and led us home. After Mom used it to lead us for several days, I lost my fear and became accustomed to the noise. Then, whenever she called us to follow, it became a game to see how fast we could run beside or behind it. When we ran faster, the ATV sped up. It soon became like a friend. Sort of like a safe companion when Mom left us alone. Some even dozed beside it at midday.

My legs were getting longer and stronger. I could take big steps as I ran. I imagine it looked like I was galloping like ponies I had seen running and frolicking together. Perhaps that is why young cranes are sometimes called "colts." My wing feathers also were growing longer and my muscles stronger. I could hold my wings straight out to help with balance as I ran.

One day our routine activities were interrupted. Mom was near the ranch house.

"It looks like trouble!" shouted Gad.

Three big dogs came out of woods by the upper pond. A black one ran ahead of the others. It looked like they might be planning to have a picnic lunch, at our expense. A half dozen of us gave alarm calls alerting the others to danger. Mom heard us, saw the dogs, and calling, began running toward our pen. We quickly followed her. After we were inside the pen, she closed the door and ran towards the ranch house.

The dogs stopped in the field we had abandoned. They seemed to know we were safe in the pen. After watching Mom leave, they turned towards the upper pasture where horses were grazing. Having failed to picnic on cranes, it seemed the dogs were frustrated and eager to take their anger out on anything they could chase. The horses watched the dogs approach until they were close, then burst into a gallop. They kicked up their hind legs, like it was a game, and raced out of sight over a hill.

A pickup truck rushed from the ranch house to the field where the horses were now beyond our view. It stopped over the hill where I could only see the top of the cab. Suddenly, softened only by the distance, I heard a half dozen "bangs," from where the truck stopped. Between the third or fourth bang I heard another unfamiliar noise, "Kie,Kie,Kie," or something similar. Soon the truck returned to the ranch house. The horses appeared at the top of the hill to watch the truck leave. They walked slowly, feeding along the way, back to the hillside where the dogs first chased them. I never saw the dogs again.

Life was not boring. It seemed like every day we learned something new. The next day was no exception.

Figure 2. A young sandhill crane. Their bill is not as thick and long as that of a whooping crane and their body is smaller.

CHAPTER 4

COUSINS?

I had seen them at a distance, following Mom, as she walked or sat on the ATV. They looked a lot like us, smaller, perhaps younger, with light brown feathers. Evidently Mom had another family. That flock did not have as many birds as ours. They lived in another pen that I could not see, but I could faintly hear some voices. I never thought much about them until this day. I had been too busy eating, exercising, growing, and learning other new things. Anyway, we were about to become acquainted.

Mom arrived at the usual morning time, on the box, followed by her other family. I hesitated when she opened the pen door and called us to follow, "Purrrep."

"Does she expect us to go exercising with those strangers?" said Lois.

"They look stunted to me," said Midian.

I was not sure how to react to these strangers. They, also, seemed uneasy about meeting us. Several of my companions, especially Ahiram, were much taller than they. I soon discovered these were sandhill cranes, sort of like cousins to us.[7]

At Mom's repeated urging, I left the pen, and moved close to the ATV and her. She seemed to want us to get used to them and to be their friends. I did not understand why. Within a few days, I and the other whooping cranes were companions with these cranes, yet not close friends. Our close friendships had formed earlier. Likewise, the sandhill cranes' close friends were among their own kind. We all got along okay and had fun together.

We whooping cranes could cover ground faster

---

[7] Sandhill cranes are found in North America, Siberia, and Cuba. Small populations in Mississippi, Florida, and Cuba do not migrate. The sandhill cranes that migrate, totaling several hundred thousand birds, nest in the northern United States, Canada, and Siberia. They spend winter in the southern United States and Mexico. The plumage of adults is slate gray in color. Sandhill cranes and whooping cranes sometimes use the same habitat during the migration and wintering periods.

because our legs were longer. The sandhill cranes usually were last in the line of birds following Mom.

At first I had trouble understanding what these cranes said. They spoke with a southern accent, or at least they sounded different. However, within a few days I became accustomed to their manner of speaking.

Although they still lived in a separate pen, from then on they went with us on all our outings to the fields. As time passed, we learned to accept and respect one another. In particular, I became friends with Izehar, who was their leader. He seemed pretty relaxed and did not appear to get excited about anything. You might say he took every- thing in stride, although his stride was shorter than mine. His different sense of humor received mixed reactions.

Like the time he said to us, "We need to party. I understand you guys know how to whoop it up." Or, when he referred to our longer necks, "You sure know how to crane your necks!" His corny humor was enough to make us moan with pretended pain. Despite that, I knew he was smart and alert.

Before long, Mom introduced us to another strange object. At first I thought it was supposed to be a bird, bigger than an eagle, and it was scary. It was white with black wing tips. It would fly at a distance from our home with Mom on it. In a few days, after I became used to this thing, she parked it beside our home. Obviously, the noise was much louder when it sat nearby.

Figure 3. Izehar, on the right, was leader of the sandhill cranes. He was smart, alert, and had a corny sense of humor.

A strong wind almost blew me over when it turned its tail towards us. We all ran to the other side of the pen. I became used to the wind after I realized it did not hurt me. Then it became a game to run across the wind, or face it, and let it blow my feathers. Later, I learned this was an ultralight plane called a Dragonfly. We named it "Big Bird" or "Bird" for short. Mom sat near the front, making it go.

When I was about six weeks old, Mom taught us to follow Big Bird as it taxied on the ground. She sat on Bird and called us. The plane went back and forth across the big field while we ran faster and faster. As I grew older, with longer wings and wing feathers, I discovered I could rise a few feet off the ground whenever I flapped my wings.

As you can imagine, the tricky part was returning to the ground if I was going too fast. My feet had to move quickly or I would lose balance and crash-land. Often it was funny, yet sometimes it hurt and bruised. Soon I learned to turn the tip of my wings forward and inward. Each wing formed part of a circle, like an umbrella, to catch the air. Then I could slow down and not lose balance as I landed. Remember, I did not have a parent crane to teach me these things.

Whenever Mom left us to do other things, Big Bird stayed in the field. Soon we were as comfortable with Bird as we had been with the ATV. Her wings made shady places to rest where eagles were unlikely to attack. It was about then that I experienced another of the gifts I had been promised by The Spirit of Living Creatures.

Mom walked up to our home with another mankind. "There they are, Hank. I lost one to a golden eagle several weeks ago. The others are fine. They do a good job of following the plane as I taxi back and forth. I'll try leading them high in full flight in a few days. I'll let you know how they do."

"Alex, when do you think you should lead them south in migration across the Rocky Mountains?"

"By the middle of October they should be strong enough. That's when the wild sandhill cranes head south from this area. We can stay away from the big flocks of wild cranes by flying west of their main migration pathway. I don't want the wild cranes attracting our birds away from following the plane."

"That seems wise. The U.S. Fish and Wildlife Service will make news releases about our progress as we move along the migration route," said Hank. I have letters ready to send to State and Federal agencies in areas we migrate through. No doubt their employees will receive phone calls, from curious citizens, reporting birds following airplanes. The letters describe our research. I want to be certain that agency employees can explain the purpose of our research. Does it look like the ultralight plane will meet the challenges of the migration?"

"Yes, the Dragonfly has a high wing, a push propeller, and open cockpit," replied Alex. "It was built in Australia to tow gliders and modified so it could fly as slow as the cranes. The average flight speed of migrating whooping cranes is thirty-three miles per hour and with a brisk tail wind they have been clocked at sixty-two miles per hour. The Dragonfly's air speed, between twenty and sixty-four miles per hour, matches nicely with the cranes' average speed. An added fuel tank means the ultralight can fly about five hours without refueling."

"Have you found anyone to accompany you in a second airplane?" Hank asked.

"Carl Logan volunteered to fly a Rans S7. It's an experimental plane with a high wing and an air speed of about ninety-nine miles per hour. Because it is much faster than the Dragonfly, it will be perfect for flying ahead. Carl will report the weather conditions my lighter plane will face and help protect against any attack by eagles," answered Alex.

"How about the sandhill cranes you are raising, are they and the whoopers getting along together?" asked Hank.

"Yes, when the sandhills were about thirty days old I introduced them to the whoopers on their daily outing. They quickly became accustomed to one another. Since then, the two groups have been combined when they are outside the pens."

"That's great! The whooping cranes experience with sandhill cranes will help them adjust when they are released this fall near big flocks of wild sandhill cranes in New Mexico. It should make it easier for the whoopers to join the wild cranes, learn what to eat, where to roost, and how to avoid danger." Hank paused as though considering what to discuss next. "Federal and State waterfowl committees have approved our research. I have the necessary permits from the State Agencies. Should I arrange a rental truck to haul our equipment?"

"I have an aircraft trailer the ground crew can use to carry tools, aircraft fuel, the portable pen, food, medical supplies, bedding, and personal gear. The ground crew will have radio contact with the pilots. They will be the first rescue and repair personnel in case of an aircraft emergency. At night we will attract the birds into the pen. Some of our crew can sleep in a tent nearby to be certain the cranes are not disturbed at night by wildlife or people," Alex replied.

"I'll see who I can get to help on the ground crew," said Hank.

"Grace, and my brothers, Ezra and Cliff, are planning on helping us," said Alex.

"Good." Hank paused as he looked more intently towards the whooping cranes. "That fairly tall bird, standing apart from the others, has been carefully watching us ever since we arrived."

Looking toward the cranes, Alex said, "Oh, it's Firstborn. He was the first chick to emerge from the egg. You know how the Bible places importance on the firstborn male in a family. He is responsible for the family when the father is absent. He receives a double portion of whatever the parents have to offer as an inheritance. Also, he has the right to spiritual leadership, like being the family priest. The fathers of our flock are not here, so I guess the first one hatched would be in charge. Oddly enough, he does seem to be developing as the leader of the flock."

"The rest of the flock seems to be busy with other things," replied Hank, frowning as though puzzled by the bird's behavior. "For some reason Firstborn seems fascinated with our every movement."

They turned and walked towards the ranch house. I was unable to hear more of their conversation. Wow! Like the Spirit promised. I was able to understand the mankind's language. Mom, who I now knew was named Alex, seemed proud of how well we cranes were following the plane as it taxied. Alex said he would be leading us flying high in a few days.

And the other mankind asked Alex when he would lead us in migration across some mountains. It sounded like we would be going south with Mom. Would we have to learn to fly like the ravens and hawks we watched from a distance? They flew really high. A chill ran down my spine. I did not like the thought of flying high. I had a knot in my stomach. I would prefer to walk! Or, unless we could ride on Bird's back like Mom did.

Are Alex and Hank the ones the Spirit said were trying to help us endangered whooping cranes? If so, I suppose they would be related to Noah who protected animals in the Ark during the great flood. And what about the others mentioned, Carl, Frank, Pete, and Grace? It sounded like they also were trying to help us!

So, Alex named me Firstborn because I was the first to hatch. I guess I'm extra special, *one chosen.* I have a right to be some kind of priest, kind of a spiritual leader. I did not realize the importance of what Mom named me, and how it would change my life. If I had known the dangers I would face, I wonder, would I have climbed back in my egg and closed the lid?

Hmmm, let's see, what was it The Spirit of Living Creatures said to me that night? Something about helping mankind form us cranes into a Team to migrate south. I did want to obey the Spirit! I wanted to do whatever was needed. Why, that would be easy. Who wouldn't want to live down south where it is warm in winter? We all loved following Mom, laughing and jumping. It was like a great game. Surely leading them would be a piece of cake, or at least a medium-sized frog. Ha! Was I ever dumb! Little did I know the dangers awaiting us when we migrated and spent winter in wild areas of New Mexico. Such wisdom would only come through experience.

CHAPTER 5

GROWN-UP TALK

I was more than excited!! I could understand what humans said!

Raham walked over to join me. "Firstborn, you look mighty proud of yourself. Like the time you caught two minnows in the stream that runs through our pen. What exciting thing did you do this time?"

Oops. I had not realized others would notice my excitement. How much should I tell her? Would Raham believe that I understood what Mom and her friend said? Or would she think I was imagining things? I better sound convincing.

"Do you remember the time I told you that whooping cranes eat mice and birds? You were surprised I would say such a thing."

"Yes, I remember. Soon after that, Ono and Aaron found those baby mice and ate them," she replied.

"Well, somehow I knew that whooping cranes eat those things along with seeds, minnows, bugs, worms, tubers, and other stuff. I knew it was true in my heart. And, did you see Mom talking with another one like her a little while ago?"

"Yes. I noticed you were watching them very carefully," Raham replied.

"I know it sounds silly, but I believe I could understand their, ah, grown-up talk. Yes, that's right, grown-up talk. You know, Mom never says much except to call us to follow her. She talked different when the other grown-up was with her."

That took fast thinking. I didn't want to say Mom was a mankind. So, I had to give some reason why she might be talking differently than she would to us young cranes.

"If I understood correctly, Mom said she was going to teach us to fly high in a few days behind Big Bird. You know, like we see ravens, vultures, and hawks fly high over the fields where we feed."

"It is hard to believe that we would fly so high." replied Raham,

"But we are cranes, cranes are birds, and birds fly high. Why shouldn't we learn to fly like other birds?" I asked.

"We don't need to fly high and it seems dangerous to me. Chickens at the ranch house don't fly high. They are birds. Quail in the fields are birds. They only fly a little above the ground like we do when we chase Big Bird. I like it better staying close to the ground."

"But, we have to learn to fly high to migrate." Oops, that word migrate just slipped out. I hadn't meant to say anything about migrating. I was too eager to convince her about learning to fly.

"Migrate? What is that?" she asked.

"Birds migrate if they live up north in summer and down south in winter. They fly between the northern and southern areas in spring and fall. Flying between the areas is called migration. They spend winter down south where food is plentiful and it is warmer."

"Firstborn, you are being silly. We don't need to fly south. Mother will give us all the food we need to stay right here."

"But, what would happen if Mom ran out of food and we couldn't find enough seeds or worms to eat?" I asked.

"You worry too much. You are a daydreamer. Let's be thankful that the Creator takes good care of us."

"I am thankful, more than you can imagine. Just remember what I said about Mom teaching us to fly high behind Big Bird in a few more days. Speaking of Mom, here she comes to take us for our afternoon exercises."

It was a good opportunity to end our conversation. I needed time to think more about what the mankind said, to consider how it would affect me and the others.

The next few days of training were pretty normal. We would spend time following Bird taxiing on the runway, a mowed area in the field. Then Bird would take off and fly a short distance above the ground. We took flight and followed for this longer, faster flight close to the ground. I enjoyed racing with the others.

We had morning training classes, followed by several hours roaming the fields, resting, and feeding on anything tasty. One morning, after our flight training, Kir discovered a quail nest containing about a dozen eggs. He was unable to eat many before others discovered his good fortune. They helped him finish this picnic lunch. An afternoon session finished the normal day's training. But, the normal was about to become a feather-raising experience.

It happened one morning several days after Hank's visit. With Mom urgently calling and encouraging us to follow, Big Bird sped up, lifted off the ground, and kept climbing. None of us cranes tried to fly much higher than a horse's head. So Bird circled and landed nearby. Then I realized this was it. Alex wanted us to fly high.

Bird taxied nearby. Again Mom called us to follow. It seemed like everyone was talking, running, and laughing. As the plane went faster, we went faster. Mom excitedly urged us to follow. I was flapping my wings and running near the front of the group with Kir in front of me. Bird sped up and lifted into the air. I leapt into the air, flapping my wings with all my strength.

Up in the air I rose with the plane. Kir slowed to a run on the ground along with the others who had been following me. When I was treetop height, I looked down. Oh my! Everything was far below me. I thought I left my stomach down there. My whole body trembled. By cupping my wings, I put on the brakes. With backward wing thrusts, I slowed to a gentle landing.

I sensed a presence, then the voice. "Firstborn, my gallant leader, what are you doing?"

"I am protecting my neck. The ground was way below me! I was afraid."

"Firstborn, you are strong, brave, and I have given you a sound mind."

"Spirit, I like the part about a sound mind. I'm happy to keep it that way."

"Firstborn, you are not a quitter. I created cranes to soar to great heights, to fly over mountains. You will also. You can overcome your fear. Show the others you are not afraid. They will follow you. Remember, I am counting on you to help mankind save your species from extinction." Then the Spirit became quiet.

Bird circled, landed, and taxied near us. Mom again urged us to follow. With the encouraging words of the Spirit echoing in my mind, I was determined to try again, no matter what happened. Like the earlier effort, we began chasing Bird. However, flock members behind me were complaining about Mom's flights.

"Why is Mom trying to get us to fly higher? I'm not going to risk my neck!" said Maath.

"Me neither. Going higher would be totally abnormal," said Abagtha.

"It might be okay for her, she is sitting on Big Bird. I don't have Bird to sit on," said Nimrod.

The Spirit said I was brave and a leader. Not convinced, but willing to try, I ran along the plane's right side as it taxied faster. When I sensed Bird was about to leave the ground, I lunged forward with my strongest wing beats.

I was surprised at my speed. My body lifted slightly above the plane. A wind gust blew me closer to Bird's body. Uh-oh! Then I was in serious trouble. I had to keep up with Big Bird's speed or her tail would crash into me. Mom was only a few feet away. She continued to encourage me. Flapping my wings as fast as possible, I was frightened enough to have extra energy. I wanted to look down, but was scared, and too busy keeping ahead of Bird's tail. Big Bird began turning left, moving away. Increasing my wing beats, along with stronger down strokes, I slipped close behind Bird's right wing.

Flying was much easier there. I could keep my position with less wing flapping. It seemed like I was getting a boost from the air disturbance behind Big Bird's wing. And, the plane's wing was protecting me from the head wind. Then I glanced down. Trees below looked like little bushes.

"That's it, Firstborn! Keep it up, keep it up!" said Mom.

Bird slowed a little and we seemed to be soaring. I could see the distant trees along the river that the great horned owl told me about. I was at an altitude equal to about halfway up the mountain north of our home. Down below, among the flock members watching us, some seemed happy and envious. Others looked angry that I was up there, perhaps thinking I was a fool or a show-off.

We made a half circle, began slowing, and headed back towards the ground. Bird was going down faster than I wanted to. The ground seemed to be rushing up to meet us. I had to concentrate on landing. So I turned away from her side and slowed my speed. I was still going too fast to keep my balance when I landed. My body was going faster than my legs could run. I ended up tumbling, toenails over beak, with the wind knocked out of my air sacs. Fortunately, my friends were at a distance over a low hill and did not see my sloppy landing. I managed to stagger back to my feet, to look cool before they came in view.

Raham spoke first. "Oh, Firstborn, that was wonderful! You looked so handsome up there flying with Mom. What was it like? Were you scared?"

"At first I was frightened. With Mom encouraging me, I began to enjoy it. The view is so beautiful. I could see a river, small patches of trees, and fields in shades of green and brown. Our world is so much bigger than I imagined. It seemed to go on as far as I could see."

By then, others were crowding around, speaking to me or to their friends. They were all talking at once, so I was unable to tell who said what.

"You looked like an eagle."

"Are you trying to take over Bird's job?"

"Who is he trying to impress?"

"Talk about being a show-off!"

"He's going to kill himself flying up there."

"I thought he looked so natural."

"No crane should be up so high."

"We belong on the ground like chickens, quail, and turkeys, not flying high with buzzards."

"He's an idiot if he goes up again."

I told them, "We cranes fly between a northern nesting ground and a southern winter area. Mom is trying to teach us how to do what comes natural for us."

"Firstborn, those things that seem natural to you are unnatural for us normal cranes," said Midian.

Most of the flock acted like they hadn't heard Midian or me. Mom parked Bird, turned off the engine, and left. I would have several hours to rest, feed, and loaf before the afternoon training. A good nap suited me fine. My shoulder muscles ached from flying. I was too tired to fly again right away.

I heard Midian talking to his friends, "Firstborn is trying to be Mom's favorite, to act like Big Bird. He's a jerk if he thinks he can impress her. He will end up crash diving if he keeps on acting like an eagle. I know better than to pull such a stunt. When brains were being passed out, he forgot to ask for some."

I ignored him. At least half of the flock thought I was a hero for flying.

Ragau walked over and stood close beside me. He was a friend to everyone, one of the kindest members of our flock, always ready to help others. He enjoyed showing his younger brothers and sisters where to find special food tidbits or how to catch grasshoppers. "Firstborn, do you think I can fly like you did?" asked Ragau.

I also wondered if the other flock members could fly high. Most were younger or smaller than me. But I remembered what The Spirit of Living Creatures told me. If I led the others would follow. So I answered Ragau, "Of course, we were made to fly over mountains. All of us can do it - if not today, at least after we grow a little more."

Soon our entire flock was busy eating. I was hungry after the exercise flying. I found a good area for seeds, to capture grasshoppers, and a few earthworms. Then shade beckoned beneath Bird's wings. I slept soundly until startled awake by alarm calls warning of danger. Ono warned us of an eagle's approach. The eagle, evidently realizing he could not make a sneak attack this day, slowly turned, drifting west towards neighboring ranches.

"Thank you, Ono, for being alert." I was relieved that my friends were safe. "As much as possible we all need to be on guard to avoid another loss like that of Nathan."

"A high five, Ono." said Deborah, as she and Ono touched each other's right wingtip. Others said "Yes" or nodded in agreement. I could tell Ono appreciated attention and praise from the others. He showed a lot of promise as one of the best flock members. Later he would prove to be one of the bravest.

CHAPTER 6

A REAL TEAM

Mom arrived at the usual afternoon time. She was too early to suit me. My wing muscles were stiff from this morning's flight and my spill. I wasn't ready to fly again so soon. However, some others were eager.

"This time we are coming with you," said Gad.

"Show us how it's done, Big Guy," replied Izehar.

I knew I needed to be an example as their leader. Otherwise they might become discouraged. Quietly I spoke, "Spirit, I need extra strength for another try at flight. Help me. Strengthen and protect the others when they try to follow Bird."

Mom looked directly at me, and then called us to follow. Evidently, she thought others would come along if I flew again. And she was right. Ono, Gad, Ragau, Aaron, Lois, Izehar, and Ahiram eagerly crowded nearby, talking excitedly about what they were about to do.

In front of the group was Raham. "Wish me luck, Firstborn."

I nodded, "May the Creator give you strength." I suppose my answer was drowned out by engine noise as Bird started down the runway.

The pause to encourage her put me at a disadvantage. I lunged forward to the right of Bird, where I had flown on the morning flight. I kept looking at an imaginary target behind the wing where I knew it was easier to fly. My feet were racing across the ground. At the same rhythm my wings were flapping up and down. Soon my speed was great enough and I left the ground at the same instant as Bird. I rose rapidly with Raham a few feet behind to my right.

"Try to fly close behind Bird's wing," I shouted as I moved closer to Bird's body to make room for her. She took my advice. With a burst of effort, she quickly moved beyond my right wingtip. I was surprised by her agility and strength. I thought females were supposed to be weak. She said nothing, but seemed happy to be so close.

I looked behind us. Gad, Ono, Ahiram, and other eager ones were scattered at various distances behind

Bird. I could tell they were struggling to keep up. Nevertheless, they were experiencing the exciting view of country far below us. It was so beautiful. Mom seemed delighted at the group following as she continued to encourage us.

"You are doing great. Keep it up!" I called to those behind. Again Bird made a wide half circle and prepared to land. I could see the remainder of our flock on the ground watching us. Perhaps some wished they had tried to follow bird. They seemed excited for those in the air.

Raham watched and copied my every move. We moved above Big Bird as she slowed for the landing, and approached the ground slower than I had that morning. With our wings curved forward, the captured air slowed our speed. I looked back. The others were following my example. Raham and I were the first to reach the ground. After several running steps, we slowed enough to keep our balance and stop. Those behind us managed to stay upright, except for tall Ahiram. He lost his balance, and went tumbling.

I was pleased at the success of friends who joined me flying. Hopefully, others would soon be joining us in the air. Except for Midian about whom I had doubts. He continued to make fun of those who had flown. He insisted flying was for fools. I wondered if there was anything I could do to encourage him. Then I decided it was not likely.

Figure 4. Big Bird is coming in for a landing. Note how exposed Mom is as she sits just below the forewing. There is no cockpit or windshield.

Mom seemed to know we were not ready for a quick repeat flight. She gave us extra time to feed and loaf before taking us on a final flight for the day. It was a struggle for me. My wing muscles were stiffening. Those friends who flew with me earlier, plus two more sandhill cranes, came on this flight.

We all looked tired when we landed. Our wingtips hung close to the ground as we relaxed our wing muscles. We must have looked like strutting turkey gobblers. I rested after the evening meal and listened to others describe their flight adventures. Later, I moved into the stream to roost and quickly fell asleep.

At dawn I was refreshed and mentally ready to go. After a hearty breakfast, I was eager to fly. However, I did need to exercise my wings to work out the stiffness. My wing muscles ached. Other areas were sore from yesterday's tumble landing. Even so, I didn't want to miss the fun of flying with Mom. Over the next two days, every time Bird went up, there were more of us following.

Finally, no one was left on the ground. Even Midian came along the second afternoon. I think he was afraid, or embarrassed that he would be the only one not flying. He was heavier than most of us and had difficulty getting airborne. Yet, he was strong, and his large wing span helped him gain speed. He soon learned flying was easiest behind Big Bird's wings. That became his favorite spot. One or two cranes were often positioned there. It was almost as though they were pulled along. Sometimes one could stay in that position with only an occasional wing beat.

After most of the flock began flying high, I seldom flew behind the wing. As leader, I believed it was necessary for each flock member to gain experience flying in various positions of the formation. I knew we would have to take turns, during long migration flights, so each one could rest behind the wing.

During our flight training we flew in the early morning and again in late afternoon. However, we did not fly if there were strong winds or it was rainy. Big Bird's long, wide wings made it dangerous for her to fly in windy weather. Also, Mom sat in the open on Big Bird. There was no cockpit or windshield to protect her from rain, wind, or bug collisions.

Summer was wonderful. Daylight lasted longer. Warm days were great for loafing in the sun after our flights. As we gained strength, Mom gradually had us flying higher and farther. Perhaps the routine and pleasant flights made us careless. One event was about to awaken us from our relaxed attitude.

It was after our morning exercise. We were returning home for a midday rest, preparing to land on our home field. Pasach was evidently happy to be home, perhaps feeling more energy than most of us, when it happened.

As we approached the landing field, I briefly saw him doing back and forth di-de-dows. That's what I call that movement which allows us to rapidly lose altitude. Both wings were cupped sharply forward to catch the wind, to slow his speed. He tipped his body back and forth like a leaf drifting down from a tree. He may have been eager to be the first on the ground. But, not in the way it happened.

I was higher, passed over him and, fortunately, did not see what happened next. I heard cries of alarm from those in the rear of the flock. I looked up, trying to see if an eagle was approaching. Quickly I glanced down to see if we would be landing among coyotes or some other danger. I was unable to see anything suspicious in any direction.

When we landed, I could tell some were in shock and grieving. Mom was running towards the side of the field we first crossed as we prepared to land. Then I saw what she seemed to be aiming for, a lump of white and rust brown with twisted black legs bent upward at grotesque angles of uselessness. We watched with dismay as Mom knelt, searched for any evidence of life, then bowed her head as if in a combination of prayer and grief. After a few moments she lifted the limp form and carried it toward the ranch house.

Dorcas told me what happened. Pasach was losing altitude rapidly. He seemed to be watching the rest of the flock rather than his own pathway. Perhaps he forgot about the line stretched between poles on the field border. If he saw the line it was too late to avoid it. The line caught him at the base of his neck, sending him tumbling backwards to crash on the ground. Other mankind arrived a few days later and buried the line so it was no longer a flight hazard.

The loss of Pasach was hard to understand. If any good resulted from this tragedy, it was that we all became more cautious when flying in areas where mankind had lines stretched between poles. We saw firsthand how deadly the lines could be. This knowledge was especially valuable later when we migrated.

As days passed we became stronger, more agile, and enjoyed our trips to surrounding areas. Mom would lead us around awhile before landing at some new location where we could rest and feed. Sometimes Bird landed directly in short grass pastures. At other times she landed on dirt roads, to park beside an alfalfa field or pasture.

Generally we favored flying in either of two formations. Our first choice, a V-formation, seemed natural for our flock size. The point of the V was centered on Bird. V-sides extended away from and behind her. Big Bird broke wind resistance for the birds directly behind her, making their flight easier. Each crane, in the sides of the V, benefited as the bird in front of it provided some shelter from wind.

A few birds were not enthusiastic about flying in formation. "The scenery does not change much unless you are the lead bird," Gad complained. "You only see the north end of a bird going south."

Echelon, our other flight formation, consisted of a single line of birds at an angle to the right or left of Bird. We preferred this formation when the prevailing wind was from the right or left. For example, if the wind was from the right, our line angled behind Bird to the left. The purpose of these formations was to preserve energy for the entire group. The formations were not critical on short training flights. Still, I knew we should conserve our energy, as much as possible, on a long migration flight.

Philetus, a name meaning "worthy of love," liked to fly beside or above Mom. These positions required the most energy because nothing sheltered her from wind's full force. Mom would talk to her with short "purrs." They both seemed to delight in the close relationship. I was concerned such a position would be too tiring for Philetus on a long flight. However, our training flights were seldom longer than one hour. Philetus had the strength needed to maintain her position for that length of time. I was certain she would have to drop back and join the rest of us on longer flights.

We learned how to land in various places avoiding trees, bushes, fences, poles, and the lines stretched between poles. We also learned to remain alert to danger while we were at these unfamiliar sites.

On one occasion we landed by a pasture where curious cows stood watching us from a distance. Our flock was scattered about the field feeding on beetles, grasshoppers, and a few grass seeds. Several were fortunate enough to capture lizards in a rocky outcrop. We had been there for an hour or longer. Mom seemed to be lying on her back, asleep in the sun, on Bird's wing. Someone gave an alarm call and others joined in.

At first I thought the approaching danger was two wild dogs. As they came closer, advancing from tall grass, I saw they were coyotes. They seemed to be checking out the chance for a good meal, watching for any crane weaker than others, injured, or somehow easier to catch. We moved away from them, towards Mom. Hearing the alarm calls, Mom hopped off Bird's wing and walked toward us. The coyotes, when they saw her, ran away.

At one field there were short grasses that looked different. While probing in the sandy ground for grubs, Deborah discovered there were small nutlets attached to the grass roots. She could probe with the tip of her bill and find them. After that, these nutlets became favorite foods whenever we were in similar sandy areas.

Figure 5. Part of the Team is feeding while enjoying a break between training flights.

Sometimes the smallest event, something insignificant in itself, can turn things upside down. It had been days since Kir found the quail nest. My memory of it had disappeared like the eggs in the nest. But, my memory was about to be refreshed.

CHAPTER 7

RAVEN'S CLAIM

After our morning flight training, a raven landed on a fence post near Kir. The rest of us were not close enough to hear their conversation. I should have known, among all our Team members, it would be Kir who mouthed off to a raven. Like his name, which means "a wall or fortress", nothing seemed to scare him. He was not about to let a raven push him around.

"Come on over here and I'll correct your eyesight, brave crane," said the raven.

"Bug off," said Kir.

"I recognize you," said the raven. "After I found a quail nest earlier this summer, you ate the eggs. I flew off to carry an egg to my young ones. When I returned, you had stolen the rest of the eggs. I found the nest first."

"I found that nest," answered Kir. "I don't believe you found it before I did. You are a liar. If you found it first you would have eaten the eggs."

"Think again, wise guy! You know I can't eat or carry that many eggs at once. In my wildest dreams I never imagined you cranes would show up at the field while I was gone. If I had known that would happen, I would have called my mate and other friends to help me get the eggs. Come close and I'll correct your eyesight for you."

"My eyesight's fine. I know a good-for-nothing raven when I see one!" said Kir.

"No, I'm quite sure you need some eye surgery. You see, I'm a specialist on the topic."

"You aren't a specialist in surgery on anything unless it's dead," said Kir. "Fly down here. I'll pluck off so many of your feathers that you'll wish you could hide your ugly body behind a bush."

"That's pretty brave talk for a runt crane. One of these days I'll dine on you like I did yesterday on a dead pig at West Ranch. I was ready to dine on your buddy, you know, the one who crashed into the line between poles. I would have if a mankind had not taken him away. Crane eyeballs are among my favorite fruits. Cranes, who follow a mankind in a plane, definitely need eye and brain surgery. I can hardly wait to do a little surgery on you, dumbo." And with that threat, the raven left, perhaps to dine again on pig.

Later, Kir came to tell me about his conversation with the raven. "Firstborn, what bothered me was the raven said we follow a mankind in a plane. He said he would have eaten Pasach, after he hit the line, but a mankind took Pasach away."

"Why are you telling me this?"

"Well, we all admire you. You are wise, are like - like our leader. And I wondered what you thought about what the raven said."

"I agree, you cannot trust ravens, and they do eat dead things."

"Well, that is not exactly what upset me. It was what the raven said about a mankind. I mean, Mom does not look quite like we do. She doesn't flap her wings when she flies. I can't see feathers on her body. Is it possible she is not our mother? That she is a mankind?"

My mind was racing. What do I do now? Should I agree with him? Should I tell him the truth? How could I answer without telling him what The Spirit of Living

Creatures told me? Then I sensed that inner voice saying "Tell the truth."

"You are correct. A mankind does care for us. We are whooping cranes." I told Kir about my talks with the blackbird and the owl.

"I believe the mankind collected eggs from mother whooping cranes," I said. "He is raising us, teaching us to fly, and how to live in the wild. He feeds us well, and seems to like us. He protected us from wild dogs. I think we are safe with him."

"But, why didn't you tell us he is not our mother?" said Kir.

"Because I thought everyone would discover the truth soon enough. I did not think it was necessary to upset our friends. Everyone seemed happy believing that Mom was our real mother."

I did not think any other crane was close enough to hear us talking. Unfortunately, I was wrong.

"I knew something was not right," said Lois as she walked toward us. "Last week, some field sparrows asked me how they could become good friends of the mankind, like we were. They wanted to be able to come into our home and eat the foods he feeds us. They wondered how we became brave enough to follow him. Then they told me about other humans who live in the ranch house, including some little ones. They said Mom was a grown-up mankind who would never get feathers and wings like we have. Firstborn what are we going to do? Should we fly away and find our mothers?"

"I have no idea where we could find our mothers," I answered. "We have a good life here. It seems wise to continue like we are. Perhaps later we will discover who our mothers are and where they live. Then we will be able to join them."

"Let's tell the others quickly so they will be eager to help us look for our real mothers whenever we have a chance," said Lois.

"Perhaps it would be best to wa--." I was going to say "wait" and let the others discover by themselves the truth about Mom.

It was too late. Already Lois was rushing off to tell her close friends. It wasn't long before this new information spread like wildfire. You can't duck if you don't see a big rock coming. And I didn't see what a problem was developing! The damage was done. Little did I know what a hornet's nest had been punched!

My friends were in small groups, scattered about the field. They all seemed to be talking at once in loud, excited voices.

"Lois said some sparrows claimed we follow a mankind. And Firstborn agreed that Mom is not our real mother. How can he say such a terrible thing?" asked Dorcas.

"Kir said a raven told him we follow a man, not our mother crane," stated Ono. "And when Kir asked Firstborn, he agreed Mom is a mankind. Actually, I have suspected for some time that Mom was somehow different than us. I guess Firstborn is right."

"Oh, this makes me so sad. To think anyone would believe sparrows or a raven. Mom is my mother. She loves me and cares for me. I will not let people say bad things about her. I used to respect Firstborn. But not now when he lies about Mother!" said Deborah emphatically.

"I don't know. Firstborn said an owl and a blackbird told him first. Then he started carefully looking at how Mom was different than us. He decided those birds were correct. Firstborn is smart. I respect his opinion," replied Gad.

"I won't listen to any more of this foolishness. Mom was with me when I hatched. She is still Mom today," said Achor.

"Let's not be quick to decide who is right, and who is wrong," said Mibzar. "We don't want to run around like a bloody chicken whose head has been cut off. Let's be sensible about discovering the truth."

"What a terrible example; a headless chicken. Oh, I feel woozy like I might empty my stomach," gasped Dorcas.

"Remember, Firstborn encouraged us to follow the mankind. He wanted us to fly abnormally high," said Midian. "He is trying to be our leader. But he leads us to danger. Remember what happened to Pasach. We should not follow Firstborn or a mankind."

Arguing lasted several movements of the sun, taking up the usual time when we fed and rested. It only ended when Mom returned for our afternoon training flight. Then all crane talk stopped. It seemed like everybody was afraid Mom would understand they were talking about her.

I was thankful for anything that would end the arguing and quiet those who were complaining about me. A few were angry because I had not warned them Mom was a mankind. Others were mad because I thought Mom was a mankind. Some believed I was lying. I wondered if these events would change my friends' willingness to follow the airplane? Would it destroy Team unity after all the hard work and training? I didn't have to wait long to find out.

Mom, oh, I mean Alex, seemed to know something was different in the flock's behavior. He seemed to sense that something had upset us. Before climbing on Bird, his eyes searched the fields and sky as though seeking something that might have frightened us.

It looked like my companions were carefully studying Mom's body. Friends who thought Alex was a mankind, seemed to be comparing him with their own body, especially noting how his was different. Other flock members, who still believed Mom was their real Mother, seemed to be looking for any of her body features that might be similar to their own. It seemed like a few of those youngest cranes, who hoped that Mom was not a mankind, were already becoming disappointed.

Midian led the group that refused to fly that afternoon. Some seemed tired from arguing and missing their midday rest. Others were beginning to suspect Mom was a mankind. I think they needed more time to decide how this news would affect their willingness to follow Big Bird.

A second group was made up of cranes now confident that Mom was a man. As a result, some said they felt uncomfortable about flying as close to him. They followed, but kept at a greater distance. Without the benefit of Big Bird breaking wind resistance, it was more difficult for them to keep up. So they quit along the way and returned to the ranch.

Only a few of us, Kir, Raham, Gad, Ono, Lois, Philetus, and I, took the usual positions directly beside or behind Bird. I was tired. I believe the others were also. So we had difficulty keeping up with Bird. I could see Alex was puzzled by the obvious change in behavior of his family. Whatever he thought the problem might be, he decided to shorten the afternoon training. After a short flight he led us home and went to the ranch house.

I think most of the Team had all the disturbing news and arguing they wanted for one day. It was quiet as we ate. Afterwards, some birds moved off to be alone, perhaps thinking about what happened. Others, in groups of two or three, talked quietly, sharing their thoughts. I was sympathetic. I remembered how I struggled to understand what The Spirit of Living Creatures told me about Mom. My companions needed time to think and rest.

Most had trouble getting to sleep. Individual birds frequently moved about instead of picking one roost spot and staying there. When they finally settled down, some cried out in their sleep. I slept soundly, but only after a few hours spent worrying about my companions.

CHAPTER 8

STORMY DAYS

At daybreak, my worship of the Creator was not what it should have been. I could not stay focused. Thoughts about events of the previous day kept interfering. I remembered what the Spirit told me. "Help the mankind form your flock into a Team to follow him and migrate … ." Now flock unity was gone. Yesterday, most of the group either refused to follow Alex or seemed half-hearted in their loyalty to this one they used to call Mom. How was I going to change their minds? Was it time to tell them about our flock's purpose? Could they stand more new information so soon? Would it further upset them and lead to more rebellion? I decided to wait and see what happened this new day.

Things went to pieces rapidly. I sensed a storm was heading our way. The northwest sky darkened during breakfast. Dark clouds raced toward us. Strong winds rushed ahead. Dust and debris blew through our pen home, ruffling our feathers. Until then, I had not realized how dry it had become without rain for several weeks. A hard, pelting rain followed as if to make up for the drought.

Stormy weather meant Bird would be unable to fly. Alex came only to feed and then lead us to fields for exercise. The first rainy day provided an abundant buffet of big worms. I also caught two minnows in the stream flowing through our home. My stomach felt ready to burst. My companions also seemed full of good organic food. Pellets in our feeding trough were not touched that evening.

Rain continued for a second day, mixed with sleet and snow, after a sharp temperature drop. My first chance to see snow was also the first hint of approaching winter. I wondered how soon Alex would expect us to migrate. I hoped there was still enough time to rebuild flock unity, to operate as a real Team.

This break from training gave my friends time to sort out their feelings about Alex. It also gave me a chance to think about how to fulfill my role as "gallant warrior." What a laugh! I sure did not feel gallant. I decided to talk with others and learn how they felt about Alex.

"How's it going? Are you ready for some sunshine after this cooler weather?" I asked a group of my friends.

"It does seem chilly after the dry spell," said Abagtha.

To see what their response would be, I decided to bring up the topic of flying. "Perhaps Alex will take us flying tomorrow if the weather improves. I need some exercise to stay trim after all the worms and minnows I ate yesterday."

"I'm not sure I want to fly following this mankind. It seemed natural when I thought she, I mean he, was mother. It is different now. He fooled us. That was not nice," answered Abagtha.

"Even though he is not our 'Mom', Alex has taken good care of us, feeding us and protecting us from wild dogs," I replied.

"Where is my mother? I want to meet her, to have her take care of me!" Abagtha said with emphasis. "I don't want some mankind stepfather!"

"I wondered why Mom seemed so, so different, so unlike us," said Ahiram. "I was not surprised when Lois said he was a mankind. Yes, he taught us how to live outdoors and to fly high. He seems sad when something bad happens to one of us, like when Pasach hit the wire. But, I agree with you Abagtha. I would like to see my mother. To see what she looks like. Is she as tall as me? What will she think of me?"

"I wonder what my mother would be teaching me if she were here? Would I have to fly so high? It's scary up there, especially when the wind is strong," said Izehar.

They now believed Mom was a mankind, yet had no fear of him. The close kinship, that existed when they believed he was Mom, was gone. About half of the flock enjoyed flying. Even if Alex was not Mom, they hoped to continue flying when the weather improved. The rest said they planned to stay on the ground. Why work hard flying behind Big Bird, that silly excuse for a crane? They said real fun was to loaf in the sun and chase bugs. It certainly looked like it would be hard, if not impossible, to re-form our flock into a real Team.

The next morning arrived bright and clear, without wind. It wasn't long before Alex taxied the plane to takeoff position. We all knew the routine. Stretching my wings, I moved up near the plane. Others joined me. But Midian, and those who planned to stay on the ground, stood back and watched.

The first flight was routine. I felt a little slow after our two-day rest, but soon picked up the pace. Alex was looking at us and those still on the ground. It was obvious he wondered why half the flock refused to fly. Soon we returned home instead of flying to a more distant location. Alex seemed intent on getting the entire flock to join in flight. Facing me he said, "What's going on, Firstborn, did half the birds forget how to fly after a two-day rest?" I understood, but didn't know how to tell him what happened.

I tried to encourage the reluctant ones to follow on the next flight. A few more joined us. But after a short flight, Alex again turned back and landed. He seemed unwilling to leave a part of the flock behind on the home field.

Turning off Bird's engine, he returned to the ranch house. He seemed discouraged by the poor showing in the morning flights.

I also was troubled and walked away from the others. "Spirit, I know I need to do something so everyone will fly. I can't think of anything that would help?"

His answer came quickly, "Tell the truth, my brave young warrior."

He said nothing more, yet I still sensed His presence. He called me *brave* and *warrior*. Yet, I only felt confused. I doubted my ability. I didn't feel brave or like a warrior. The truth might not be received well by the others. I knew what I was supposed to do. But, I was afraid! Would they believe me? Or, would they make fun of me, call me a daydreamer with a big imagination? Most of my friends had not scattered to begin feeding. They were standing around talking. I needed to act fast. I had to get them to pay close attention to what I must say.

I turned, walked towards them, and said quietly, "Creator, fill me with your Wisdom and give me the words to speak." I still felt the Spirit's presence, but He did not speak. I remembered the night He promised to help me in times of special difficulties. In my opinion, this was such a time. I stopped in the group's center, near Ono, Kir, Gad, Raham, and Philetus. Being close to these friends gave me courage.

"My friends, we need to talk about something important. What we do today may determine whether our species survives. Certainly it will affect our children, grandchildren, and our own happiness."

My words seemed to get their attention. To me, my voice sounded high-pitched and squeaky. My legs felt like they were turning to rubber. I hoped no one noticed my wing feathers were shaking. Fortunately, my nervous trembling may have been hidden. A light breeze was ruffling the feathers of everyone.

"What is a species?" asked Dorcas.

The proper answer seemed to come from deep within me, from that gift of the Spirit. "A species is a group of animals that look alike and share a common name. We belong to the species called 'whooping cranes.' Whooping cranes used to live in many places, but this is no longer true. Mankind hunted our forefathers for food and drained the nesting marshes to make more farm fields. Fewer than two hundred whooping cranes now live in the only wild flock."

I heard mumbled complaints from my audience. I was not sure if they were angry that mankind ate our forefathers. Or maybe they were concerned that so few of our kind remained. I was pleased that they were listening carefully. I decided to continue talking before they had a chance to ask more questions.

"Our species nests much farther north in the Northwest Territories in a place called 'Canada.' In winter, there is not enough food to eat and it is very cold. So they fly south in the fall to spend winter in a warmer place called Texas. A hurricane or a disease outbreak could kill all of them while they are concentrated in Texas. If that happened, our kind would only remain as captives in pens.

"Mankind wants to start wild flocks in other locations. Then our species will have a better chance to survive in the wild. This flying from one place to another, in spring and fall, is called 'migration'. Young cranes fly south with their parents in the fall. Along the way they learn the migration pathway to their winter home. In spring, following the same flight pathway, the young fly back north with their parents. If necessary, however, the young can find their way back north without the help of their parents.

"So biologists wondered how they could start new populations. They knew it would not work to trap adult cranes, and move them to a new area. The adults would simply fly back to their familiar home area. But young cranes, raised in captivity, might offer a solution to the problem. Perhaps they could be taught to learn a new migration route.

"Mankind has some adult whooping cranes, including our parents, in pens in other locations. Some of their eggs were removed so we could be raised in this place. When we were little we followed Mom like other crane chicks instinctively follow their mothers. The mankind we thought was our 'Mom', his name is Alex. He taught us to follow the ATV, and finally to chase after Big Bird. His goal is to teach us a migration route. If the experiment is successful, we will have helped him create new locations where our kind can nest and spend winter. Then our species will be safer, less likely to disappear from the wild."

"Wait a minute," interrupted Midian. "What kind of fairy tale are you telling today?"

"Please, let me finish. Then I will answer your questions." I tried to ignore Midian and speak to those who were good friends.

"Yeah, let him finish. I'm hungry and want to go eat!" said Nimrod.

"We have been given an important job. Our Creator wants us to help mankind start a new flock of wild cranes. Soon, when weather turns cold, Alex will lead us south with Big Bird to teach us a migration pathway. Next spring we can follow the same route back north. In the future we will be able to start a new flock of our kind and raise our families around here. We will be helping our species survive. That is why we are here without our mothers and fathers."

"A fantastic story," said Midian. "I can already guess how this fairy tale ends. I wouldn't want to wake you from your imaginary dream. So, we shall all leave now and go eat lunch."

And he walked away, believing the others would follow him. But, he was wrong. Some seemed to be curious about what I said and wanted to ask questions. Others didn't believe me and wanted to argue. I was glad to see Midian leave. Among those who might disagree with me, I believed he would be the most critical or argue more than the others. I could see him picking half-heartedly at plant leaves as though eating. When no one followed him, evidently he was too proud to return and listen to our conversations.

"Firstborn, let's all fly to where our mothers and fathers are held captive. We can help them escape. Then we will start a new flock with our parents," said Philetus.

"I don't believe that is possible. I don't know where our parents are. As long as we thought Alex was Mom, we followed him. We still need to follow him south to learn a migration pathway to a winter home. First, he has to continue training us to migrate behind Bird. It has never been done before. If we return north in spring, without the assistance of mankind, the experiment will be a success. It will provide a way to start other new flocks of our species."

"I refuse to help mankind do anything," said Aaron. "Why should we? You say our parents are prisoners in pens and mankind took their eggs! Alex tricked us into believing he was our mother. Why should we follow him? We can stay here in winter."

"I understand your anger. Yet we cannot spend winter here. We would die. When it gets cold there will not be enough food to eat. The mankind's Bible says '[Even the migratory birds are punctual to their seasons.] Yes, the stork [excelling in the great height of her flight] in the heavens knows her appointed time [of migration], and the turtledove, the swallow, and the crane observe the time of their return.'(Jeremiah 8:7a) You see, the Creator even speaks of us cranes and migration. Please, ask some of the other birds around here. Most of them migrate in fall. They told us the mankind was not our mother. I'm sure they will also tell you that we must migrate if we want to stay alive.

"More importantly, we will be migrating to make certain our species survives. It would be terrible if we whooping cranes only lived in captive pens. Don't you want to be sure we have children and grandchildren who live free? Alex has been taking good care of us. I believe he wants to help us. Shouldn't we help him? Most of all, we should obey our Creator, the one who made all things. We should help our species."

"Whooping cranes, eh, how do you know so much about our history? Who told you what mankind is trying to do? Did other birds tell you?" asked Nimrod.

"Some things I seem to know by instinct. The Spirit of Living Creatures visited me one night. He asked me to help form us into a Team to follow mankind and migrate south in fall."

"That's unbelievable. You claim some Spirit talked to you? What makes you so special? The Creator does not have time to be concerned about what happens to us," said Mibzar.

"Wait, that is not true! The Creator's book, the Bible, says 'Observe and consider the ravens; for they neither sow, nor reap, they have neither storehouse nor barn; and [yet] God feeds them.' (Luke 12:24a). Aren't we of much more value than ravens?"

Mibzar did not answer. Many of my friends murmured "Yes." They seemed to agree that we were better than ravens. However, they had no idea what the Creator's book said, and obviously found it hard to believe my claim that I was visited by something called The Spirit of Living Creatures.

I don't think it would have helped to tell them what mankind's Bible says about other animals who received special instructions from God. Like the large fish that swallowed Jonah to take him to a place called Nineveh (Jonah 1:17; 2:10), ravens sent to feed the prophet Elijah (1 Kings 17:2-6), a donkey given the ability to see an angel and speak to his master Balaam (Numbers 22:21-33), wild animals who obediently entered Noah's ark (Genesis 7:1-3), and lions' mouths closed when Daniel was thrown into their den (Daniel 6:19-23). And what could possibly cause mother cows, to abandon their nursing calves, in order to return the Ark of God to Israel (1 Samuel 6:7-13)? God's personal attention even included a gourd plant and a cutworm in the life of Jonah (Jonah 4:6-7).

My friends had no knowledge of the Bible, God's Love Letter to mankind. They also lacked the special knowledge about other things that The Spirit of Living Creatures shared with me. What could I say to convince the others we needed to migrate following Alex and Big Bird?

CHAPTER 9

FLY OR DIE

Then, Raham spoke up. "I trust Firstborn. Several weeks ago he told me that we are whooping cranes. He said sometimes we even eat things like baby birds and mice. I could not imagine eating a mouse. But Ono and Aaron ate baby mice they found in a mouse nest. They said mice tasted fine. Later, Kir and others found and ate quail eggs. Firstborn told me mankind soon would be teaching us to fly and to follow Big Bird. A few days later it actually happened. He is a brave and valiant leader. I don't understand how he knows all these things. I do know he is truthful. And I want to help save our species."

"I agree," said Kir. "Firstborn was the first one to know Mother was a mankind. He was the first to be brave enough to fly high with Bird. He has been our leader all along. If following Bird will help our species, our children, and grandchildren, then I will follow."

"Let's go ask the other birds about this thing called migration and whether it is safe to stay here in winter," said Achor.

"Good idea," said Nimrod. He and several others flew in different directions to talk to other birds. The rest of the group was hungry, yet still thinking about what I said. More talk could wait. They chose to find something to eat. Later they could find out what Nimrod and Achor learned after talking with other birds.

I was relieved to have a chance to eat. I needed to think more about how to encourage my friends to follow Alex and continue our training.

"Raham and Kir, thank you for your support and friendship."

"Firstborn, I am proud of you for being a brave and valiant leader," said Raham.

Whoops, there were those brave and valiant words again. I seemed to have to live up to that description. I fed for about an hour. Too excited to rest, I walked over to where some of my friends were talking.

"Firstborn, you are right. The wild birds say we must fly south before winter. There is nothing to eat when cold temperatures and deep snow arrive. They say we will die if we do not migrate. What should we do?" asked Aaron.

"We must continue our flight training so we will be strong enough to migrate. Help me encourage the others to continue flying. There must be enough of us to start a new population that will nest in this area and spend winter wherever Alex leads us. Then we can help keep our kind living free in the wild. We need a safe place to raise our children and grandchildren."

"We will help," they chimed in. And help they did.

In midafternoon Alex approached and started Bird's engine. I quickly moved into the flight position. I was pleasantly surprised. Evidently the word had spread quickly. We could stay here and die or fly south this fall. I did not know if anyone believed The Spirit of Living Creatures had spoken to me. Nor did I know how many believed we would help save our species. What they believed did not matter to me as long as we followed Alex south this fall. I wanted to obey the Creator.

Only Midian, and two others, failed to follow when Bird took off. When we were airborne, Alex looked back and saw the increased numbers. Calling, he flew Bird in a wide circle. With all of us encouraging them, the remaining three joined us. "Yesssss!" I was delighted, filled with the joy of success. We could still be a Team working together with one goal. We would help save our species. And, I would be able to obey the Spirit.

In the next few weeks we took longer flights to new landing sites. Air temperatures dropped and light snow covered the ground at daybreak on several days. We became stronger. Most Team members were courteous and willing to take turns so their tired friends could also rest behind Big Bird's wings.

One morning, Alex and another mankind entered our pen. They carried boxes of supplies and a long pole with a net on one end. One by one they caught us in the net. I don't believe anyone enjoyed that experience. Our feathers were pretty ruffled when it was over. They gave us a "health exam" to be certain we were well enough to migrate.

A plastic leg bracelet, with a small radio transmitter, was placed on one leg of each of us. Some transmitters were powered by the sun and the others by something called batteries. Each transmitter gave off a different signal. Alex had something called a "receiver" that allowed him to hear the transmitters' signals. These signals made it possible to identify us up to a mile away, or to find us if we became lost.

The bracelets had black numbers or letters on a bright yellow background. The black markings made it possible for Alex to tell us apart when he watched from a distance through the two-eyed thing called binoculars. My bracelet was a nuisance. I pecked at it, but was unable to remove it. After several days I became used to it and it seemed like a natural part of me.

Flocks of Canada Geese and ducks were passing overhead, flying south. Hawks and eagles migrated through the area. Some smaller local birds had already departed for warmer places. I knew our day to migrate would soon arrive.

Figure 6. A plastic identification bracelet, radio transmitter, and black antenna were attached to a leg of each crane.

Two days later another small plane landed. Until then, we had not seen other planes except at a great distance. Alex walked out to greet the pilot, Carl, who had volunteered to join us on migration. His plane was faster than Big Bird. He would fly ahead to see if weather conditions were suitable for Big Bird to fly.

Alex led us on a training flight. Carl followed. We were frightened by anything as big, or even larger, than an eagle. I had not forgotten what happened to Nathan. I did not like it when Carl came close with his plane. We all crowded up beside or below Bird. When nothing bad happened, after awhile we returned to our flying formation. Evidently Alex wanted to see what we cranes would do when Carl's plane was nearby. Later, when we migrated, I became used to seeing Carl's plane. But, we were still frightened when unfamiliar planes approached.

Things were different one afternoon in mid-October. There was no training flight. We were not released to feed in fields. Perhaps we were being rested before the big migration flight. I could hear sounds of trucks arriving and other activity near the ranch house. Carl flew in with his plane. At dusk, Alex gave us an extra portion of food, which I appreciated.

As I prepared to go to roost, I was confident about what the next day would bring. Earlier I heard one mankind say the word "praise." I wondered what it meant. Suddenly I became aware of a similar word from the mankind's Bible. "I will confess and praise You ... for the awful wonder of my birth! Wonderful are Your works, ... My frame was not hidden from You when I was being formed in secret ...." (Psalm 139:14-15). Whoever wrote that understood God's creative ability. That night was pretty cold, but I stayed warm due to my layering of feathers, thanks to His creative design in me.

Dawn was different than any others I had experienced. The sky seemed a brilliant blue. Frost on the field looked like a white crystal gown glistening with the sun's reflection. I sensed excitement in the air. Lark sparrows were chattering about some migration adventure that awaited them. Blackbirds, congregated in one large flock, swooped back and forth, up and down, like waves at a lakeshore. They landed briefly, only to burst forth again, like another wave.

Alex fed us a lighter meal, but did not lead us from the pen. Whatever he had planned, he made sure we could not exercise too much or overeat and become lazy. He paused before returning to the house.

Facing our Team he said, "Today we start our big adventure. I'm counting on you to perform. You will fly higher and longer than ever before. We begin an 800-mile race against bad weather and danger. It will take every bit of strength and courage you have. Still, you will see God's creative beauty like never before. He will guide our flight."

His words sent a cold chill, a forewarning of danger, down my backbone. There was a serious tone in his voice I had not sensed before. His voice expressed concern and respect. His face showed the same tenderness we saw when he lifted Pasach from beneath the line.

When he finished speaking, he seemed tense. He stood looking at us. I sensed a depth of appreciation and love. A close bond had developed over our months together. He seemed to drink in the unique qualities of each one of us. After a few moments he turned and with firm steps walked back toward the ranch house. I thought I should tell my companions what Alex said.

"He said that today we will start on an adventure, flying higher and longer than ever before. For 800 miles we will race against danger and bad weather. We must be strong and courageous. We will see new wonders of God's creation. He is counting on us to perform and the Creator will help us."

Most of the others seemed to be thinking seriously about what I said. Midian gave a scornful laugh. "Firstborn claims to understand the words of mankind. He is a warlock, a sorcerer, a worshiper of the evil one. He imagines he has special magic to know what mankind says. What kind of trickery is he up to now? I knew all along he could not be trusted!"

I ignored him. I knew the truth of what I said would be proven later.

Raham responded, "Remember, weeks ago Firstborn told me he heard Alex say he soon would teach us to fly high. It proved to be true. I believe he is also correct this time. And, oh, didn't you sense Alex's love for us?"

"Poorly placed trust, Miss Raham," said Midian, bitterly.

Philetus said, "Firstborn, what do you mean, he is counting on us to perform?"

"I think perform means to do a good job, to fly strong and hard, keeping up with Big Bird. Simply doing whatever Alex asks us to do."

"Oh," Philetus said with a firmness that confirmed she would do her best to perform for him. She, unlike other flock members, always flew close to Alex when we were airborne with Bird. Even after she knew Alex was not her mother, she still flew alongside, above, or in front of him.

"How far is 800 miles?" asked Gad.

"I'm not certain; I know it must be a long way. Much farther than our daily flights that I heard Alex say were about twenty-five miles."

"What will make it so dangerous?" asked Aaron.

"I don't know. I suppose things like eagles, lines between poles, coyotes, bad weather, and perhaps other things we have never experienced."

"What does racing mean?" said Abagtha.

"That's like when we try to see who can run or fly the fastest. The fastest one wins. Alex said we would be racing against danger and bad weather," I replied.

Somehow, to migrate had a new meaning. Before, it seemed like a fun adventure. A vacation to somewhere not visited before. A restful journey when we might make new friends. Or a visit to interesting places. Now it seemed like dangerous, hard work, a test of our strength and courage. It could be a scary time when we would face unknown dangers. Migrating had lost some of its attraction. I remembered the encouraging word the Spirit said about assisting me whenever there were special difficulties. It was a comforting thought, and also would be in the future.

CHAPTER 10

TAKEOFF

Big Bird had been parked in the field. At daybreak, her wings glistened with a heavy layer of frost. But now, with the sun higher in the sky, her wings were dry. Carl and Alex walked towards Carl's plane the Rans S7.

"I'll fly ahead. In five minutes or so, I'll call you on the radio and report whether wind conditions are suitable," said Carl.

"Do you have the shell crackers?" asked Alex.

"Yes, I placed them in the cockpit. I hope they'll do the job. I test fired a few using a sawed-off shotgun. They go out thirty or forty feet before exploding. The bang and flash should frighten any eagle that tries to attack the cranes."

After Carl checked the cockpit instruments, his plane sped down the field to officially begin our adventure. His plane was always the first to take off and check flying conditions. His flights were important because mountain winds can vary over short distances due to rugged land surfaces, and changes in elevation. Later, he radioed Alex saying the wind speeds were low enough for Big Bird to fly. Alex started Bird's engine. When everything was ready, our pen door was opened and he called us to follow.

"This is it Team, let's do it," I said.

But Midian and Achor were slow to leave the pen. I suppose Midian was being stubborn. Achor seemed afraid. We ran behind Bird, calling, encouraging one another. Some were excited shouts to encourage themselves and their friends. Other calls seemed meant to release nervousness and to express bravery.

"Let's show the mankind what we were designed for," shouted Ono.

"Come on, Ono, you move like an old goose," said Gad.

"I'll be down south to greet you when you come staggering in," replied Ono.

"We finally get to show our stuff and stop loafing on these little training flights," bragged Izehar.

"Those mountains won't have time to blink when I turn on my afterburner," said Nimrod.

"Watch out, Nimrod looks like a hummingbird on permanent overdrive," laughed Lois.

"Big Bird will be following when we get going," added Ragau.

"Yes, following in a cloud of dust," agreed Deborah.

Down the runway we raced with Bird, gaining speed, until suddenly we were airborne. I saw Alex look back, and then turn Bird. Part of the flock hesitated at the takeoff. They lagged some distance behind and below the rest of us. We circled, reduced our altitude, to allow the slower group to catch up. Then Alex headed south.

Once underway, the flock became quiet. Each one seemed to concentrate on their thoughts, or on saving energy. Philetus was in her favorite position near Alex. We flew in V-formation with the youngest birds behind Big Bird's wings. I was midway back on the left arm of the V. Raham was ahead of me. The outer arms of the V were made up of the stronger or more adventurous of the flock, including our sandhill cranes. The first area we flew over was familiar from previous training flights. Gradually we entered a large valley. Below we saw greater numbers of cars, trucks, and mankind's buildings.

Ahead, I occasionally saw Carl's plane. Below we were followed by mankind's ground crew in three pickup trucks, with one pulling a trailer. Other mankind noticed our flight overhead. Cars and trucks pulled to the roadside. People stood outside their vehicles and homes watching the unusual sight of large birds following a plane.

I began to think about the days ahead. They would test whether we were prepared mentally and physically. We were expected to migrate in a manner different than wild cranes. When wild whooping cranes fly south they take long flights mixed with stops for days or weeks to feed and rest. Our flights would be more like a marathon race. Each day we tried to make progress toward our final goal. Also, Big Bird was unable to fly at the slow speeds typical when cranes spiral upward in air updrafts. We needed to maintain faster, flapping flight so Bird could safely make wide circles. I believed our Team was ready for the challenge.[8]

---

[8] Whooping cranes normally migrate at altitudes between 1,200 and 5,400 feet. In average conditions they travel 250 miles in seven to eight hours or about thirty-three miles per hour (E. Kuyt, *Aerial radio-tracking of whooping cranes between Wood Buffalo National Park and Aransas National Wildlife Refuge, 1981-84.* Occasional Paper Number 74, Canadian Wildlife Service, Edmonton, Alberta, 1992, 53 pp.). Wild cranes use flapping flight, the up and down wing motion, for normal flight speeds at average-altitudes. They save energy when warm air updrafts are available. These columns of warm air, like invisible elevators, help to uplift the birds. Within updrafts, the cranes spiral in tight turns upward, using some flapping flight to help gain a favored altitude. Then, with wings extended horizontally, they glide towards their goal, slowly losing altitude. Eventually they may enter another warm updraft and again spiral upward.

Our morning flight was uneventful except for a brief scare. A sandhill crane thought a distant plane was an eagle and gave the alarm call. Some dodged beneath Bird's wings and body, using her as a shield. Others scattered towards the ground. Midian apparently left us about then. We soon properly identified the object as a plane and reformed behind Bird. No one noticed Midian was missing until we landed in fields near an auxiliary airport.

Although Carl searched, back-tracking over part of our route, he was unable to pick up a signal from Midian's radio transmitter. Perhaps Midian was too far away, beyond the signal range. To be honest, I knew I would not miss Midian's critical comments. And that made me feel guilty. I knew I should have been more concerned about his wellbeing. Later, we learned that he returned to our ranch home where Alex's father opened the pen door for him.

We loafed and fed until late afternoon. Our landing site was not visible to most mankind. Some strangers knew about our presence, and a few watched us from a distance. I could see Alex and others talking with these visitors. They did not approach closer and that was fine with me. Except for Hank's visit, and the health exam, Alex had been our only close contact with humans. I was curious about other mankind. Yet, I also was a little fearful, fear learned from the behavior of other birds towards men.

There was a light breeze. Conditions seemed okay for a late afternoon flight. Soon Alex started Bird, called to us, and away we went. I could see a high mountain range in the distance. It looked like our flights would be especially challenging the next few days.

At dusk we flew beyond a small town and landed beside an alfalfa field. The ground crew assembled a portable pen and fed us. Throughout migration the pen was our nighttime safe haven, providing safety from coyotes, dogs, and owls.

Figure 7. The Rans S7 and Big Bird are parked in a field while part of the Team relaxes nearby after the first day of migration.

Alex checked something called a Global Positioning System (GPS) before telling the ground crew we had flown another sixty-four miles. I was tired even though most of this flight had been over fairly level terrain.

That night, Hank and Carl slept nearby. It took me several days to become accustomed to having men nearby whenever we were not flying. Despite their presence, I fell asleep quickly. However, my sleep was troubled. Over and over I dreamed I was struggling to keep up with Bird. As night moved into day, my body resisted the change. Both body and mind voted time should stand still so I could sleep a little longer.

CHAPTER 11

AERIAL COMBAT

Fortunately, dawn came slowly. Whisper Mountains to the east did not seem willing to release the sunlight. They acted like a door slowly opening to the sunlit sky, allowing it to enter my darkened side of the mountain. My body feathers were covered with frost. I shook myself. Frost crystals glistened in the air, drifting to the ground. As they picked up their sleeping bags, Hank told Carl the air temperature was twenty degrees, whatever that meant.

Our flock was beginning to stir. Raham was still sleeping with her head tucked among side feathers. I gently tested my wing muscles. No problem. They were not stiff. Our training had been sufficient. My body was not sore after the first day migrating. I thanked Creator for our progress and safety.

A few companions were slowly walking in the pen, drinking from a water container, looking for any food item overlooked the previous evening. Only nearby alfalfa leaves were found for a morning salad. No one seemed in a hurry to start the day. The planes were parked nearby, their wings covered with frost. Big Bird could not fly until her wings were dry. Alex brought breakfast, but did not release us from the pen. Perhaps he did not want to risk having any of us take off before the planes were ready.

The men began wiping frost off the planes, checking the engines, adding fuel. Two more mankind arrived to assist on the ground crew. The sun had been up awhile when we finally took off on Day Two of our adventure.

After gaining altitude, I had a better look at mountains seen the previous evening. Sunlight glistened off yellows of aspen leaves and reds of oak brush. These colors contrasted with bright greens of pines and dark greens of spruce and hemlock. Streams on mountain slopes, shaded by trees, looked like ribbons that danced downward. A light blue sky held only wispy clouds. It was a beautiful day, yet, the huge mountain ahead looked angry, unwilling to let us pass without a fight. I felt uneasy when I realized our pathway led over it.

Some time passed before the cause of my concern became evident. We had to constantly flap fly to rise up the mountain's height. We were flying up a canyon with cliffs rising high above to our right and left. A moderate down slope wind added to the difficulty we had keeping up with Bird.

Spook, the smallest member of our flock, especially found it hard to keep up. Ragau, dropped back to fly alongside and encourage him.

I called to them. "Come on Spook. When you can catch up, I'll get you a position of rest behind Big Bird's wing." I was hoping he and Ragau would double their efforts. But, it looked like Spook had no extra energy to give.

Figure 8. The moon is still visible at daybreak of Day Two as dawn arrives slowly. Carl's plane is anchored to the ground in case strong winds arrive. The wings are covered overnight with waterproofed canvas to make it easy to remove ice, snow or a heavy frost.

The distance between us was increasing. Alex noticed their difficulty. But on this forested mountain slope there was nowhere he could land so Spook could rest. We continued, struggling to reach the mountain pass.

The next time I looked back, Spook and Ragau were about ten plane lengths behind and much lower in altitude than the rest of us. I had been watching for eagles high above us. A warning would give the entire Team enough time to avoid their diving attack. But noone saw the pair of golden eagles until it was too late. They must have been sitting on some cliff ledge, partially hidden, waiting for prey. Gad saw the two in a power dive from the right side of the canyon. "Look out, eagles!"

We dodged beneath Big Bird or scattered below. Most of us had not seen the eagles. I was not scared because on our first day there had already been several false alarms about eagles that turned out to be distant planes.

I looked back. "Oh, - no!"

Several others saw what I saw, and cried out in distress.

"Watch out!" shouted Mibzar.

"Dodge, Spook!" commanded Ono.

"Look out, Ragau!" screamed Lois.

"Poor Spook," said Raham sadly.

I was startled to see the powerful force as the eagle's talons crashed into Spook. There was a cloud of feathers looking like something had exploded. Perhaps Spook never saw what struck him. Tightly gripped in eagle talons, his neck limp, together they headed for the earth's surface. It was over so quickly. I hoped Spook did not suffer.

Others, seeing Ragau dodge and twist with the second eagle close behind, continued screaming alarm calls, "Look out! Look out!"

Alex called Carl on the radio, shouting something about eagles. Carl's plane, ahead of us, turned sharply, and passed overhead as he searched for the eagles.

Alex called us to follow, trying to get us reassembled behind Bird. I hesitated, wanting to fly back to see if I could do anything to help Ragau. However, I realized my first responsibility was to lead. If I turned back, it would add to confusion and might endanger others. We needed to stay with Alex and let Carl deal with the eagles.

"Come on. We need to follow Bird to find a safe landing place," I said.

That was the only instruction needed. Those who had scattered, or were still beneath Bird, reformed and continued up the mountain. With the eagle scare came a fresh burst of energy that made flying easier.

Soon Carl's plane rejoined us as an escort. Quiet, constantly alert, and fearing another attack, we quickly traveled the last few miles to Golden Pass. I grieved for

Spook and worried about Ragau. It was a great relief when we landed.

Carl joined us and said, "I saw an eagle eating one of our birds on the side of the mountain near where they attacked. I was unable to find the second eagle or the other crane."

"I never saw those eagles above us. They must have been sitting on a cliff waiting for migrating birds to bring dinner," replied Alex.

"They certainly had an ideal spot to ambush birds that could not land in trees. The victims' flying speed would be slow as they climbed in altitude. There was no place to escape," said Carl.

"These eagles may be a greater danger than I thought. Except for the young crane killed this summer, I only know of one other time when a crane was killed by an eagle. As they say, we'll have to keep an eagle-eye out for them. I sure hate to lose any of our birds. They are like good friends. Besides, I spent so much time raising and training them. It cost a lot of time and money to get them to this age and flight condition."

Both men were quiet for a few minutes. They seemed to be deep in thought.

Alex broke the silence. "Flying conditions are ideal for making a long descending flight from this high pass. We should take advantage of the weather as soon as our birds rest awhile."

"I'll contact the ground crew after we are airborne," said Carl. "There was no road for them to follow directly beneath our flight path. They took another route and are waiting up ahead."

"I'll have Matt and Sonju return to where the eagles attacked. They should be able to recover the radio transmitter from the dead crane. I hope they can find the other crane, number forty-nine, and lead him back to us."

After resting awhile we again took off. Carl flew above and behind us in an ideal position to quickly stop an eagle attack. In my opinion, anything flying above us might be an eagle. Sometimes, when I glanced back, and saw Carl's plane, I was momentarily startled. I still had to get used to his following above us.

We had a good tailwind and pleasant weather. We passed over beautiful forests and countryside, while gradually losing altitude. It should have been a pleasant flight, but was not. I was upset by this morning's tragedy and constantly watched for other eagles. Some Team members began to pant as the air temperature increased at lower elevations. Alex noticed some might be overheating and decided to end our morning flight. Everyone seemed happy to be back on the ground.

Matt and Sonju returned from their search. I hoped to hear them give Alex a good report about Ragau.

"We found the radio transmitter where Carl saw an eagle feeding on a crane. The eagle's talons pierced through the crane's rib cage into the heart. The body was partly eaten. We saw no eagles and we were unable to hear a transmitter signal from the missing crane. Perhaps it escaped from the eagle and was too far away for us to receive a signal. Or, if it was killed, the sun-powered transmitter may have been blocked by debris and was not transmitting."

The news about Ragau was not what I had hoped to hear. I chose to keep the bad news to myself rather than further upset my friends. Wind delayed our takeoff until late afternoon. We flew awhile before landing at dusk near an isolated wetland. We were able to feed in a wonderful marshy area. It was exactly what we needed to take our mind off the morning tragedy.

The marsh edge offered an abundance of nut grass. Soon we were probing into the ground for these nutlet delicacies. They were a welcome change from the pellets that mankind fed us. One mankind described the pellets as a "high protein dog food." The pellets were filling, evidently healthy for us, but dry, and without the gourmet taste of natural foods.

"Thank goodness for organic foods," said Ono. "I was afraid I would start barking, chasing cars, marking my territory, or who knows what other terrible thing. Just in time I have been saved by getting something to eat besides that fancy dog food."

A few steps farther into marsh led to another discovery. Mibzar was chasing young frogs to quench his hunger and thirst. Several of us joined in this sport. Obviously, no raccoon family had discovered this abundant supply of delicious snack-size frogs. Low purring noises, which signify good feelings, became the main sound from our Team.

A few more steps of my long legs took me into deeper water where minnows might challenge my aim. One did; I missed. The speed of my bill thrust pushed through the soft marsh bottom into something hard that remained stuck to my lower bill. Cautiously I tasted this piece of plant tuber.

"Huh!" This might be worth further study. Probing gently with my bill tip, I pulled a tuber from the plant. Why it has a smooth malt flavor blended with mustard seed, ground blueberry, and a dash of wild onion. "Hmmmmm."

Raham moved closer. "What did you find, Firstborn?"

"Wait a wing beat while I see if I can find another." I looked at plant leaves where I found the tuber. A similar appearing plant was nearby. Searching the marsh bottom I pulled a tuber free and offered it to her.

She seemed especially pleased. "Why, thank you," she said and quickly accepted the morsel. There was a long pause as she considered this culinary surprise. "Ummmmm. It tastes like ground blueberry with a touch of wild onion and a smooth malt flavor blended with mustard seed."

Her taste reaction was like mine! I guess I looked surprised, because she said, "What's wrong?"

"Nothing, your taste description was similar to mine. I guess great bird brains have similar food tastes."

"Oh, silly you, what will you think of next?"

What would I think of next? That was a thought to consider!

"I don't know what we should name this food. Look, there are other plants like it. I believe I will try a few more."

All in all it was an interesting evening dining out. At dusk we heard a pack of coyotes announcing their hunt. Their sound was enough to remind Alex to call us to the pen.

CHAPTER 12

A NEW DANGER

At dawn of Day Three, I had no idea how far we had migrated. In my mind, I kept a roadmap picture of mountains and rivers along our pathway to help me return north the same way next spring. I wondered if we might be near the end of our migration. Then I heard Alex speaking to the other mankind.

"We covered 179 miles in two days. At that speed, in about five more days we should reach the cranes' winter home."

That was exciting to hear. But it had been a costly start with three of our Team already dead or missing. I had seen another dangerous-looking mountain in our pathway when we landed the previous evening. I hoped it would not be as challenging as the last one.

Figure 9. In the evening of Day Two we had a well-deserved break at a wetland. Deborah is in the upper left, Philetus in the center and Dorcas in the foreground.

After our energizing evening meal, a good night's rest, and a beautiful sunrise, we were eager to start. No one spoke of yesterday's tragic loss; or their fear. I was proud of them. Hank was ready to release us from the pen. To our Team I expressed my hope for this day's flight. "Here's to the survival of our species."

"For the survival of our species," others firmly responded. From that day forward it became our battle cry when we started flights. It gave us courage and deeper purpose to face the dangers ahead.

"And for the life of our children and grandchildren," added Abagtha.

This day's flight was unlike our long, climbing flight of the previous day. We were too close to the mountain to allow a direct climbing flight. Instead, we flew in wide circles to gain altitude. I understood this spiraling upward when I saw the full height of those steep mountains ahead. We stopped our circling climb when it appeared that a direct flight would allow us to clear the mountain pass. Carl was circling behind us. I heard him on the radio, "Alex, I haven't seen any sign of eagles."

"That's good, we need a break from that problem!" replied Alex.

As we approached closer to the mountain slope I felt greater air resistance. It was like an invisible power slowing our progress. We were entering a stream of cool air flowing down towards the valley we left. There it replaced warmer air rising above farm fields. The wind felt like big rocks on my wings and back. Alex increased power to Bird's engine, once, then again. She inched upward, roaring with new-found effort. Although slowly gaining altitude, we were still being pulled into the mountain.

Some of my friends were panting heavily, lagging behind. I called out loudly, "Abagtha and Deborah, let Mibzar and Dorcas trade places with you so they can rest awhile behind Big Bird's wings."

Then I heard Alex calling on the plane's radio, "Carl, this downdraft is pulling me towards the mountainside. I may not have enough power to pull free. If I can't reach the top of the mountain, I'll have to try to land on the highway."

The road was the only landing spot in dense forest below. Only a few straight stretches would provide enough length for Bird to land. Trees along the road made it barely wide enough for Bird's wingtips to miss branches. It would take Alex's excellence as a pilot to avoid trees in the twisting current of this wind. I also wondered how he could find a place to land between trucks and cars racing up and down the highway.

Our flock had become a confused, unorganized mass. Weaker fliers were trailing way behind, forced towards the ground. Some were making distress calls of fear as they felt the weight of wind rushing towards the valley. It was like an invisible hand forcing us into the mountain. Airflow speed increased as we approached the mountain. I could see tops of pines, bent and twisted with the wind, like angry, ugly faces, daring us to crash amongst them.

The full fury of fallen nature seemed against us, but we struggled on. The scene of Spook, limp in the eagle's talons, flashed across my memory. Anger mixed with grief, added fuel to my determination. The barriers thrown at us had the signature of the evil one. Our strength was the Greater One, but we were only beginning to appreciate the dangers we faced.

It was the Creator's desire that we succeed. We were selected and His Hand was upon this journey. Without that assurance I would have given up. I sensed the mankind felt the same way. I heard Hank discussing it between flight sessions. We cranes felt privileged to help restore our species to a more secure position in this fallen world. It would be worthwhile even if it took a super-bird effort.

I needed to be brave and provide leadership. Creator's love would keep us together to the end, but some of the Team were fearful, tired, and losing hope. I moved to the rear of the flight and increased my wing beats, turning my head to get a full view of the air space above and behind us. A careful search assured me there were no eagles preparing to pounce on us.

"We'll have to land in the road," I shouted to be heard above the wind and Bird's engine. "We have no choice. Watch out for mankind's cars."

I could see Lois and Maath, those trailing farthest behind, were already landing. Two cars, coming uphill near Lois, were stopping at the unusual sight of cranes in front of them. A truck, coming downhill around a curve, swerved around Maath, then continued without stopping. Other companions were preparing to land.

"As soon as you land, move to the roadside," I shouted.

Those flying behind Bird's wings were still keeping up. However, I was afraid they would be in danger when Alex maneuvered to land.

"Move away from Big Bird," I instructed. "Alex may have to quickly change directions when landing."

Friends were making distress calls as they were forced to land. Bird's engine strained at maximum power. Treetops seemed to be beckoning her to disappear within them.

"Ono, lead the others. Find a place to land between mankind's road traffic."

"Right-oh, Firstborn" Ono shouted. His name means strong and one who has energy from God. Then he, and those still following Bird, dropped back, cupping wings like parachutes, to slow their descent.

"Gad and Izehar, follow me and do what I do," I instructed. These two, among my bravest and strongest fliers, obeyed immediately. It took all of my strength, and I'm sure, an equal effort of my two companions, to keep up with Bird.

Alex seemed to be trying to pick a straight stretch of road, without cars, where he could land. He tipped Bird's wings up and down, signaling cars he needed to make an emergency landing. Then we were near treetop height. Wind, roaring through trees, almost drowned out sounds of Bird's engine. She slipped right as we cleared some taller trees. The road was straight, seemed long enough for landing, and was clear of traffic. It sloped uphill, so Alex should be able to land in a shorter distance. But landing upslope, instead of on a level runway, would be tricky.

Alex lowered Bird into an avenue between trees that blocked the wind. With that protection, it appeared to be easier for Alex to maneuver Bird. He was preparing to land. The roadway beneath was clear of cars. Suddenly, a car rounded the curve ahead, racing directly towards Bird. The driver had a startled look on her face. It looked like a head-on collision could not be avoided. Bird's engine strained one more time. Her wheels barely cleared the roof of the car that never slowed in downhill flight.

Bird dipped back toward the road. I wondered, was there still enough straight stretch for a safe landing? I hoped so, but I had other problems to deal with.

"Gad and Izehar, cut across that curve up ahead and land where you can block any traffic coming downhill towards Big Bird. I'll drop back and try to slow a truck coming uphill. We need to protect Alex and Bird."

Without answering, they rapidly passed over trees to land on the next uphill stretch. I turned up, sharply right, extending my wings to catch the full force of the wind. It pushed me over towards a road curve where a semi-truck would soon enter the stretch where Bird was landing. I tipped from one side to the other, reducing the air support beneath my wings, losing altitude rapidly. Quickly, I was in line with the approaching truck's windshield.

The truck driver's surprised look indicated he feared some crazy bird might come through his windshield to join him in the cab. I banked sharp left, avoiding the truck's cab, zipped alongside the truck, and landed gently some distance behind. With a grinding noise, the huge truck came to a stop after the driver had his first view of Big Bird. I was safe for the moment. That's when I finally realized the danger of the last few minutes and the energy required. I felt dizzy. My legs became weak. I staggered back on my hocks, beside the road, until my heart rate slowed.

Cliff soon arrived in a chase vehicle. There were places he could drive around trees to reach Bird. Then he served as an escort. He led Big Bird past other vehicles pulled off between us and the summit.

Gad, Izehar, and I joined the parade to the top. We were worried about the safety of Teammates along the road below us. We did not know another chase vehicle was rounding up the others. They joined us at the summit. The entire Team was shaken by our life-threatening experience. Fortunately no one was injured.

Raham spoke to Gad, Izehar, and me. "Oh, I am so happy to see you are safe. Why didn't you land with the rest of us?"

"We needed to stop any cars that might hit Big Bird when she was landing," I said. Gad and Izehar landed uphill to slow traffic coming downhill. I believed drivers would be surprised to see unusual birds on the road and would stop. I landed downhill from Bird for the same reason."

"There is a little bird statue on the front hood of Carl's old truck," said Gad. "I thought Firstborn might become like that. It looked like he was going to land on the front of a huge truck. I guess the driver thought a bird was going to crash into him. Anyway, it caused him to stop before his truck reached Big Bird."

"Oh!" Raham looked frightened at the thought of stopping a truck.

I am confident she was not as frightened as I felt when I was heading for the truck windshield.

Alex led us walking across the summit of Frozen Pass. Nearby a meadow and stream were hidden from the road. He evidently thought we deserved a good rest. We all agreed.

It was pleasant in the meadow. The sun warmed our backs. A few friends were soon napping. Some made repeated trips to the stream to quench their thirst after this morning's difficult flying. Others began chasing the large noisy grasshoppers that fly about on warm fall days. The mankind were resting or working on equipment. Later I caught a few minnows in the stream. Nimrod ate a small lizard. It was a peaceful spot.

We spent the night there even though we had not traveled far on Day Three. I hoped we had put behind us the most difficult and dangerous part of our journey. During the night, I heard ducks talking along the stream.

A great horned owl visited awhile, sitting on Big Bird, but did not announce his presence. I had a restless night, sometimes half-awake, sometimes dreaming I was struggling against the wind and chased by a monster truck.

CHAPTER 13

WINTER STORM

Someone said the elevation at Frozen Pass was 8,000 feet. This high elevation improved the likelihood we could make a long flight on Day Four. Being eager to get underway, we were airborne before Bird. Alex quickly took off and moved into the lead. Most of our flight was over beautiful forestland. Later, we passed over drier land, with dark green sagebrush scattered on brown earth. Wind increased as the morning progressed.

Then we were attacked by two golden eagles. Ahiram gave the warning. We all reacted immediately, diving beneath Bird for safety. One eagle, approaching from above, at first showed no fear. Alex turned Bird up, approaching the eagle head on. At the last possible moment, to avoid a collision, the eagle turned away. Alex continued to chase it while we scattered towards the ground.

Carl turned his plane across the flight path of the second eagle as it tried to attack. He fired a shell cracker towards it. The explosion was enough to make the eagle pause. Our flock landed near a small stream during the aerial eagle battle. We were beginning to feel like seasoned warriors, confident that Alex and Carl would protect us.

Alex landed nearby after the eagles left. He called Carl on the radio. "I never imagined the eagles would be so bold. Did you see the one heading straight for me? I didn't expect to be playing the chicken game with an eagle."

"I saw the eagle out of the corner of my eye. It was pretty close when he turned away from you. Either he was shortsighted or anxious to dine upon crane. His mate seemed only half frightened by the shell cracker I fired. I thought I was going to have to shoot again. It finally circled up and left."

"That frontal attack certainly increased the heart rate," said Alex. "Let's take a break here. See if you can guide the ground crew into this area."

Carl helped the chase vehicles find us. Later, Alex noticed one of Bird's wheel supports was bent during the landing on rough ground. He and Carl took it to the nearest town for repair. By the time they returned, in late afternoon, it was too windy for an evening flight.

Air temperatures dropped rapidly after dark. I sensed a big storm was on the way. My internal forecasting system proved accurate once again. Snow started falling about midnight. Large moist flakes deadened sound and hid anything that was more than a few wingspans away.

I could tell when it was dawn, but only because there was a lighter background to the falling snow. After checking tie-downs for the plane and pen, the mankind spent most of the day in the aircraft trailer, trying to stay warm. Netting over our pen was threatening to collapse on us due to weight of the wet, sticky snow. Occasionally, the mankind left their shelter to shake snow off the netting. Despite the cold, one of them seemed happy.

Raham turned to look at me, "The mankind is not making a usual noise, Firstborn, what is he saying?"

"On the first day of our migration, I heard one mankind remark about a similar noise another mankind was making," I replied. "He called it singing. To the one singing he said, 'Let the birds do the singing.'"

"Is there a message in the singing or is he worshiping?"

"Raham, I suppose you could say there is a message. It doesn't seem like worship."

"Then what is the message?" she asked.

"He sang, 'All God's creatures got a place in the choir.'"

"What is a choir?" asked Raham.

"I believe it's a group of individuals who sing together," I replied.

"And was there more to the message?"

"Yes. I can't remember all the words, but it sounded something like this. 'All God's creatures got a place in the choir, some sing low and some sing higher, some sing out loud on the telephone wire, some simply clap their hands or paws, the little birds sing, and the hoot-owl cries, the duck quacks, the honeybee hums, the cricket fiddles, the donkey brays, the pony neighs, the bullfrog croaks, and the old cow goes moo.'"

I paused, thinking about the song's words. "I suppose the message is that the mankind thinks all of the animals worship the Creator Who made them."

"What a wonderful message. I hope to hear him sing it again," Raham replied.

The storm continued without letup. I shook myself. Snowflakes that had accumulated on my back drifted to the ground. Raham was quiet awhile and I thought our conversation was over.

Then she spoke again. "Do you believe the Creator has time to think about each of us?" Her tone of voice suggested that she seriously doubted God would care about her, but sincerely hoped He did.

"It certainly sounds like He thinks about each of us," I answered. "The mankind's Bible speaks about the Creator and says 'You open your hand and satisfy every living thing with favor' (Psalm 145:16) and 'He gives food to every creature.'" (Psalm 136:25a).

Raham did not reply. She seemed to be deep in thought, perhaps considering what the Creator might think about her. Soon, being unusually quiet, she turned and walked to another corner of the pen.

Our food rations were increased, but the waiting was tiresome. There was nothing to protect us from the storm's brute power. Days Five and Six passed. The wind seemed as strong as ever. I became increasingly impatient as snow depths increased. Nothing indicated the storm was decreasing.

We paced nervously until the snow surface blended with dirt. I didn't know I could be so bored! Anything that could be pecked, except each other, had been pecked. Friends started to act pretty grouchy and impatient. Those who welcomed the chance to rest, when the storm began, now were anxious to continue our migration.

We talked about those things of interest to cranes.

"I sure would like to eat a few little frogs, or some quail eggs. Anything would be better than this dog food they call a 'special' crane diet," said Ono.

"I can still taste those delicious baby mice," Aaron replied.

"Even big grasshoppers or several earthworms would help," I agreed.

"I'd settle for grass seeds and nutlets sprinkled with ladybugs," said Philetus, in a tone of voice indicating she preferred a dainty diet.

"I would rather be fighting another down slope mountain wind than sitting in a snowstorm for two days," said Gad.

"Be careful what you wish for. We might have some more mountains to pass over," I replied.

"I wish the storm would pass," Raham said in a firm voice as though uttering a prayer. Then her voice dropped to a sad whisper. "And, I especially wish Ragau would suddenly fly in to rejoin us."

That thought about Ragau caused several minutes of silence.

"Yes, that eagle attack was a bummer. Maybe Ragau somehow got ahead of us and will be waiting when we get to the winter site," Ahiram noted in a hopeful tone of voice.

"I sure hope so," agreed Dorcas. "He was always so friendly and helpful. He was trying to encourage Spook."

"The first day's flight was a picnic compared to the last five. Anyway, who decided we had to migrate?" grumbled Mibzar.

"We all agreed, don't you remember?" replied Lois as though correcting him. "We wanted to help our species, to benefit our children and grandchildren. There is no point complaining about it now."

"I hope this storm stops, and we find the rest of the trip much easier," said Gad.

"I'm hoping along with you," Ono agreed.

"Even though our mother turned out to be a mankind, we had it pretty easy growing up on the ranch," said Maath.

"Following Mom brings back special memories. Watching Ahiram stumbling around in the grass was always good for laughs," I replied.

"Hey, I was not clumsy. I was too tall for the rest of my body," Ahiram said, and then chuckled as though he could picture how awkward he might have appeared.

"Thank goodness, you finally became coordinated before coming on this migration," said Gad.

"Another benefit of being tall is that I'm higher above the cold snow than the rest of you," Ahiram replied.

"Oh, to have some warm air temperatures like we had last summer at the ranch," said Lois.

"Do you think we will ever meet our real parents?" said Izehar, looking at me.

"Who knows?" I answered. "I can't imagine what they'll look like."

"I hope they're happy and don't miss me too much!" responded Izehar.

"I hope the remainder of the migration is all downhill," piped up Ono. "No more mountain climbing for me. I would like a strong tailwind to push us to our winter home. No more snow or rain. Only sunny days with our favorite foods at each stopping place."

"Boy, are you dreaming!" was Mibzar's discouraging reply.

"I might as well hope for the best," Ono responded.

"Hope away!" Mibzar said.

"What do you imagine our winter home will be like?" asked Maath, as though the talk about the challenge of more migrating was too depressing.

"I suppose like the ranch with a stream where we can drink and roost at night. And fields full of good foods, earthworms, sunny days, no more flight training. A pleasant place where we can relax and not worry about crossing the next mountain or dodging eagles," said Raham.

"Surely such a paradise must be why we signed on for this trip," said Nimrod in a sarcastic tone of voice.

That last comment seemed to dampen the enthusiasm for further discussion as a large group. The Team separated into twos and threes for more private talks.

I was bored out of my gizzard and yearned for some natural food instead of those fancy dog pellets. Mankind also acted like they were tired of the forced delay. They seemed as anxious to get underway. Occasionally one or more individuals left their shelter from the storm and walked about as though looking for something they might do to diminish the storm's fury. When nothing changed, they rejoined their companions inside the trailer.

CHAPTER 14

EAGLES AND COW PIES

Fortunately, Day Seven dawned with a promise of better things. Snowflakes decreased and finally stopped. Winds, high above the earth's surface, seemed to be pushing the clouds to some unseen place. The storm was followed by calm air.

When the storm began, the men had placed cloths over the planes' wings so they would remain free of ice. They began clearing snow from the aircraft, vehicles, field road, and eventually, from a homemade runway.

Hank released us from the pen while Alex and Carl were busy preparing the planes. We quickly moved into areas where mankind had removed snow, stretching our wings and legs, searching for food. There was no food.

At least we were able to move about and exercise muscles stiff from disuse and cold. Plane engines were started so they could warm up. No one rushed to take off before Bird did, as we had on Day Four.

Alex told the mankind he hoped we could travel as far as the Broad River. Carl departed and soon Alex began calling us to follow. Team was slow, taking off from scattered locations, gently calling upon muscles not yet fully limber. Alex was patient, understanding our stiffness. He circled slowly until we were assembled in tight formation off each wing. Fortunately, there was little wind resistance. After we reached a suitable altitude, the flight was fairly easy, although bitter cold.

Philetus was in her usual position beside Alex. I thought she would be unable to maintain such a difficult flying position during the long migration flights. She had proven me wrong. In previous flights she flew against the full force of wind. Nothing seemed to tire her. She had a lot of muscle in her small body.

After 30 minutes of flying, our muscles felt normal again. Everyone seemed to be feeling good. Chatter up and down the formation indicated the Team was relaxed and alert. I looked across at Raham flying in formation off the right wing. Something did not seem right. When I realized what it was I had to chuckle. "What's wrong, Raham?"

"My feet are cold, Firstborn. I'm warming them!" she said rather defensively. "What's wrong with that?"

"Not a thing. It looks funny. Normally, when I have a side view of you flying, I can see your legs stretched straight back." Instead her legs were folded forward, tucked against her belly feathers.

Others, hearing us talking, saw how Raham warmed her feet. Several friends were soon caring for their feet in a similar manner.

Throughout the morning's flight pathway we had gradually been moving to lower elevations. Everybody seemed ready for a rest. Finally, sunshine beckoned on a green field. It proved to be an excellent place to rest and eat.

Alex landed on a country road and taxied beside the field. We were soon enjoying alfalfa salad greens and miscellaneous bugs. The landowner arrived, wondering why two planes, followed by birds, landed beside his property. After Hank explained the project's purpose, he seemed relieved, and pleased to have us as visitors. He left, only to return later with young and old friends, to take pictures of the planes and us.

I overheard Hank and Alex considering an afternoon flight. However, after camping in the blizzard the previous three nights, the mankind voted for something called "a hot shower, soft bed, and warm food." For us, that night proved to be the most comfortable since migration began. Temperatures remained above freezing.

The sky was clear at dawn on Day Eight. No wind greeted us. Team seemed to be feeling good, anxious to get underway, and physically fit. I was thankful for their eager attitude. We made a wide spiraling flight to gain altitude and pass over a high mesa. Alex radioed the ground crew to tell them we were at 5,900 feet of altitude, making good progress.

Later, a warning cry "Eagles!" shattered my daydreaming. We scattered, making a more confusing target for eagles, and headed towards the ground. There were three eagles. Alex pursued one while Carl chased and fired shell crackers at the others.

After the eagles left, Alex noticed we were panting due to the warmer temperatures and excitement of the eagle attack. He decided it was time to land and told the other men that we had flown sixty-eight miles in two hours.

I eagerly drank when water bowls were offered. Our afternoon home was a dry mesa top, far from the activities of man. It was obvious that some cattle had pastured there. Grass and weeds were clipped off close to the ground. This barren mesa offered us almost nothing in natural foods. Only a few small grasshoppers tempted us to look for other foods.

"Look what's beneath these," Ono said. That attracted the attention of those near him.

The "these" were what mankind calls "cow pies," dried deposits left by cattle. They were scattered over the mesa surface. Ono broke one up with his bill, and flipped over pieces. Underneath were beetles and other small insects.

Even a small amount of natural food was appreciated. We scattered over the field to take advantage of these new-found, but limited, foods. It didn't take us long to finish this sparse buffet. Mankind set up the pen, covering it with something to provide shade. The Team soon gathered there to feed on our usual pellets.

"I'm so tired of eating these dry pellets. Oh, for a bunch of earthworms like we had at the ranch. Or moist frogs like we found in the marsh on Day Two of our migration," said Mibzar.

"Stop whining about food. Mankind will think we want more pellets. I'm tired of seeing them in our feed trough," said Achor.

By late afternoon, some friends were asking me if I knew what mankind planned for an afternoon flight. I had not heard it discussed. I also found this place boring and was anxious to move on. The sky clouded up and there was a light, cooler breeze suggesting another weather front would arrive at night. We took off rather late and had not flown long before it was getting dark. The sun slipped behind clouds on the western horizon. Alex seemed to be having difficulty finding a safe place to land.

I was anxious to land when we finally saw a field that promised a reasonably smooth surface. Big Bird slowed and lost altitude as Alex headed for midfield. Most of us stayed close behind Bird. But a few of our flock decided to land at the closest field edge. Cupping their wings they lost altitude quickly in their eager approach.

Behind me I heard, "Whoa! Look out!"

My friends landing near the field edge almost collided with one of those lines stretched between poles. They avoided it at the last possible moment. It was difficult to see because of the fading daylight. The line blended with the drab ground color. The near tragedy was a good reminder. We needed to be cautious when landing in unfamiliar places.

The weather forecast apparently warned of strong winds. As a precaution, the mankind used rope to attach the walls of our pen to stakes pounded into the ground. The planes were anchored to trucks that also shielded them from the wind. Early evening was pleasant. After they ate, the men sat around a campfire talking. I was too tired to listen and fell into a deep sleep. Strong winds awakened me later as a weather front arrived. Dawn of Day Nine revealed a covering of snow. The wind had not weakened.

"The wind is thirty-five miles per hour, with gusts of fifty," said Carl. "The Weather Channel reported a wind shear at 2,000 feet altitude.[9] It does not look good for flying." I was disappointed at another delay. We were learning patience and slept a lot. It was bitter cold on the night of Day Nine. Two men slept outside the trailer. They put on extra layers of clothes and foot coverings before entering their sleeping bags.

---

[9] Wind shear refers to a change in wind speed or direction with height in the atmosphere. It can also refer to a rapid change in winds over a short horizontal distance.

Quiet air announced the wind had departed on Day Ten. The clear sky indicated it would be a good day to fly. After gaining some altitude, we discovered the winds were still rough, but not enough to cancel the flight. Eagles came towards us three times during our flight of a few hours. A family group of three, a single, and later another single headed in our direction. They were seen at a distance and when Carl's plane turned towards them they left without delaying our flight. We landed near Monte Mesa, Colorado.

That afternoon I heard the mankind discussing our progress to date. It was about 290 miles to Bosque del Apache National Wildlife Refuge where we would spend winter. Alex said we had already completed migration over the mountainous areas where winds and weather could be more unpredictable. The remaining flight south should be easier. I was pleased to hear about our progress and the possibility of an easier flight ahead. I told the others what I heard.

The afternoon flight was an easy one as we covered another forty-three miles to land in New Mexico on part of the Navaho Indian Reservation. I was unable to find any natural food in this dry area. Our presence attracted many who were curious. We were moved into the pen to avoid problems. One mankind family "had never seen turkeys like us. Were we for sale and good to eat?" The question about eating us sent a chill down my backbone.

The Navaho people have a deep appreciation for nature and conservation. They expressed great interest in what Hank and Alex were attempting to do through the research. I was happy to tell the Team how the Native Americans admired the project. This increased our pride in what we were doing to save our species. I drifted off to sleep, wondering where were my real parents? What would they be doing at that moment? Perhaps they also would be proud of me and the Team's efforts to help our species.

CHAPTER 15

BIRD'S HORNED TOAD

Strong winds delayed our departure until almost noon on Day Eleven. When we were able to take off, we gave a one hundred percent effort. Later, the winds began increasing again and we were panting from the difficult flying. Headwinds eventually became so strong that it was necessary for Big Bird to land. The ground crew briefly halted traffic to allow the planes to land safely along a highway in northern New Mexico.

The holding pen was quickly assembled and we were attracted inside with water and food. Alex seemed to want us secure in the pen because the planes and birds were attracting a crowd. I was tired, so it was easy to rest in spite of people looking at us and asking questions. I slept after drinking and eating.

The strong wind continued until evening so our afternoon flight was a repeat of the morning effort. Later, as we continued flying, I could see the sun was setting. In normal conditions we had enough light to fly quite awhile after the sun went down. But darkness seemed to arrive quickly on this evening, aided by a heavy cloud cover blocking the western horizon. However, that was not the main reason the flight was much briefer than expected.

Suddenly Bird's engine sputtered, then quit. As Alex said later, he quickly glanced at the small instrument panel and flipped a switch changing to the second fuel tank. The engine coughed back to life, but continued to sputter. I was flying near Big Bird and could hear the radio conversation.

"Carl, I must have carburetor trouble or a plugged fuel line," said Alex. "The engine quit on me. I lost quite a bit of altitude. I managed to start it again, but it's running rough. It won't let me accelerate. I can't see anywhere to land. From your altitude, can you see a landing place ahead of me?"

"I can't see anything level that does not contain brush or small trees. Do you think you can keep Bird running for awhile?" Carl responded.

"I'll try, but it's sputtering and coughing. I'm still losing altitude."

Big Bird sounded like she swallowed a horned toad, it was halfway down her throat, and wouldn't come up or go down. There certainly appeared to be a problem.

"What's wrong, Firstborn?" asked Raham.

"Big Bird has engine trouble. Alex is trying to find a place to land."

"Is there anything we can do to help?" she asked.

"I don't think so," I answered.

"Alex, I see a pasture ahead, but there are scattered desert shrubs in it," said Carl. "The ground looks pretty rough, partly eroded."

"Is it straight ahead? I can't see it," Alex said anxiously.

"It's more to your right. It must be hidden from your view by the mesa."

"Carl, I see the mesa a little above my altitude, but I don't think I can get Bird to accelerate enough to clear it. There is nothing below me except cedar trees."

I sensed the urgency in Alex's voice. Still wondering if there was anything I could do to help, I suddenly sensed the presence of the Spirit. That quiet inner voice seemed to say, "Tell your companions to worship me. I inhabit the praises of my creation."

"Raham, pass the word down the flight line. Tell everyone to worship the Creator."

Down the flight line the instruction went. In a moment, we were calling, like at morning worship time.

Bird's engine ran smoother and, as a result, she was able to gain a little altitude.

"Carl, can you hear me? These cranes suddenly started calling," said Alex. "I can hardly hear myself! The engine is running a little smoother. I was able to gain some altitude. It looks like I will be able to clear the mesa. But I still can't see the pasture."

"It's about two o'clock from your position. I think I see a faint outline of a rutted road through it, but it's not straight," replied Carl.

We continued to worship, loudly glorifying the Creator. A few minutes passed and the daylight continued to fade. "I'm above the mesa now, clearing the treetops by about ten feet. Can you still see me?" asked Alex.

"I reduced my altitude. I can see the road better now," replied Carl. "It's to your right and runs diagonally across the field. There's one tall cedar to the left of the road beyond a barbed wire fence. If you swing more to the west in your approach you should be able to see it."

Bird's engine was sputtering more and again began to lose altitude. Alex turned the plane slightly westward. "I think I see the cedar tree you mentioned and can barely make out a fence. I'm taking her in."

We became quiet, knowing Alex and Bird were committed to land.

"You are heading in properly," said Carl. "It's too dark now for me to see the field road from my altitude. You should be on it on the other side of the fence."

"I see it. Here goes."

Big Bird's engine quit completely as she passed over the fence. Her landing was not graceful. With a few bounces, and dipping back and forth of the wings, she finally rolled to a stop.

We flew over Bird and landed in the field. Ono was one of the Team closest to me when we landed. "Firstborn, why did you have us start worshiping when Bird was choking?"

"I don't know; I just thought praising our Creator would somehow help Alex land safely. And Bird's engine did seem to run better while we were worshiping," I answered.

"It did seem to give Big Bird a boost, but was sort of spooky," said Ono, looking puzzled. "That's the first time I worshipped when it wasn't at daybreak."

"Thank you, Creator," I said quietly to myself.

By then it was too dark, and Carl's plane too high. He could not see what happened on the ground. "Alex, are you okay?"

"Yes, the landing was like bull riding at the rodeo. Even so, Big Bird held together," Alex answered.

"What got into those cranes? They were making so much noise I could hardly hear you," asked Carl.

"I don't know. That sure was weird!" said Alex. Then he paused as though struggling to find an answer. "They never acted like that before. It was almost like they thought their calling would give the plane a lift, or something." He paused as though thinking further about what he just said. "Where are you going to land?"

"I saw a good field a few miles back. I'll have one of the ground crew meet me there," replied Carl.

"Right, see you in a little while. I've had enough excitement for one day. We'll have to clean the carburetor and fuel lines in the morning. I need some shut-eye before the challenges of tomorrow."

CHAPTER 16

ALMOST THERE

On Day Twelve we were still on the Navaho
Reservation in New Mexico. Takeoff was midmorning.
We were in the air several hours. Bright sun glistened off
the yellow leaves of cottonwoods bordering streams.
Most of the countryside was dry pastureland with
scattered dark desert shrubs and sparse grasses. Our
Team was operating as smooth as feathers on a duck.
We flew in V-formation, occasionally changing positions
so each one had an opportunity to rest behind Big Bird's
wings.

Carl saw two eagles at a distance and frightened them
away using shell crackers. Later he was following behind

and above us when a biplane crossed between his plane and Bird. Alex shouted some choice words in the radio. Frightened by the plane, we scattered, dropping a great distance in altitude. The biplane left the area without a goodbye. Our flight recovered, however the air temperature was high. I was getting hot. Alex noted our panting and landed on a remote part of the Laguna Pueblo Indian lands.

Someone saw Bird go down in the distance and reported "a plane down" to the Laguna tribal police. Two officers soon arrived.

"Are you okay? Someone saw your planes go down and reported it to our office."

"Yes sir, everyone is okay," replied Hank.

"You are trespassing on Laguna Pueblo Indian lands. Are you having aircraft problems?"

"No, Officer. The planes are running fine. These birds are whooping cranes, a species in danger of becoming extinct. We are leading these captive-raised cranes in migration as part of a research project. They started panting in this heat. They needed to rest and get a drink, so we landed," said Alex.

"I need to see some identification from the persons in charge of this project."

Alex and Hank handed items to the officers along with a paper that I suppose explained the purpose of the research.

"Sir, your office can phone the numbers listed on the paper," said Hank. "U.S. Fish and Wildlife Service personnel will be able to confirm our identity and the purpose of this research. I apologize for our unexpected visit. This area seems so remote we thought our landing would not disturb anyone."

"How is leading the birds in migration going to help save them from extinction?" asked the second officer.

"Young cranes learn a migration route from their parents. We have been leading them southward like their parents would. We will release them on a wildlife refuge in New Mexico. If they return north in spring, without assistance from humans, the research will have identified a way to start a new migratory population of these cranes," said Hank.

"In these remote areas we always have to be careful about aircraft involved in illegal transport of drugs. What are the birds carrying in those little packages on their legs?" said the first officer, smiling.

Alex laughed, and said, "Those are small radio transmitters. They send a signal we can hear with a receiver. If a bird gets lost we can follow the signal until we find the bird. There are no drugs involved."

The other officer asked, "How long do you plan to stay here?"

"Only a few hours to rest and eat lunch," said Alex. "Then we will be heading south toward Bosque del Apache National Wildlife Refuge."

After examining the planes the officers seemed satisfied. They wished the mankind good luck and left.

Our late afternoon flight was another easy one. We landed at dusk in an isolated area west of Los Lunas, New Mexico.

Hank and Alex spent the evening informing television and news media of our location and planned arrival at the refuge, about seventy miles away, the following day. The weather forecast indicated good flying conditions for our arrival in late morning.

The mankind talked about this refuge where plant and animal life was protected on a large area of marshes, ponds, woods, and farm fields. The refuge certainly sounded big because in winter it was visited by 17,000 sandhill cranes, 30,000 snow geese, thousands of ducks, hundreds of Canada geese, bald eagles, and many other kinds of birds. Whatever those numbers meant, it sounded like quite a few. And, at the end of our migration, we might be greeted by some mankind celebrating our arrival.

The welcoming did not excite me. Still, I was proud we had done something that others found interesting. Perhaps it would benefit our species.

I decided to tell the Team what I overheard. "Listen up. The men believe tomorrow's weather will be good for flying. We should reach the place where we will spend winter, a place called a wildlife refuge.

"The men seem excited and have been telling others about the end of our migration. There may be some people there to greet us. I know you are all pleased to be near the end of our difficult journey. We can be proud of what we have done for our species. Remember to look sharp tomorrow. Other mankind will be watching us. We want to show them our beauty as we fly and land at Bosque del Apache National Wildlife refuge.[10]. It will be good for our species."

Everyone started talking excitedly at once. I was unable to tell who said or asked what.

"Firstborn, how close are we?"

"What will it be like at this refuge place?"

"Who will be watching us?"

"Will Alex stay with us?"

---

[10] Bosque del Apache National Wildlife Refuge is part of the National Wildlife Refuge System managed by the United States Fish and Wildlife Service. It is located in central New Mexico, bordering the Rio Grande, about seventy miles south of Albuquerque. Containing over 57,000 acres, it provides a key wintering area for sandhill cranes, geese, ducks, and a wide variety of other birds. The refuge staff manages habitat by prescribed burning, plant control, moist soil management, farming, and water level control in impoundment ponds.

"Do we have to fly over any more mountains?"

"What if eagles attack when we are trying to look sharp?"

"Will there be wild dogs at the refuge?"

"Do they have natural foods there?"

I answered, "The men say we will reach the refuge after a short flight. There will be lots of other birds there like sandhill cranes, snow geese, Canada geese, and ducks. The refuge is a place where humans take care of animals and plants. I don't know the answer to your other questions."

The excited conversations continued as the Team separated into twos and threes discussing this news. I moved apart from the others.

"Creator, I thank you for helping us reach this point in our journey. Thank you for believing in me as a leader." I sensed His presence and rested in it. The weight of leadership of the past few weeks lifted. I was filled with joy as His love covered me. Several minutes passed.

"Firstborn, you look so relaxed and happy," said Raham.

"Yes, I am. It seems so good to be near the end of my job in leading the migration. It feels like a heavy stone has been lifted from my back."

"You even look younger. What do you want to do first when we get to the refuge?" she asked.

"Oh, I may ask the wild sandhill cranes about the best places to eat and to roost at night. And, maybe I will catch up on some lost sleep."

"I hope Alex stays with us," said Raham. "I want the refuge to be like our home in Montana with lots of earthworms when it rains, alfalfa and wheat fields, crickets and grasshoppers, sunny days and warm nights. I hope we will have a pen to enter at night for safety, and extra food from Alex whenever we need it."

"I hope it has cool, clear streams where I can bathe and catch minnows," I replied.

"I wish we were already there," Raham said excitedly.

"That would be nice. I guess we'll just have to be patient. Let's get a good rest tonight so we will be ready for tomorrow's flight." And with that suggestion we both became quiet, looking at the moon and many, many stars, until sleep overcame us.

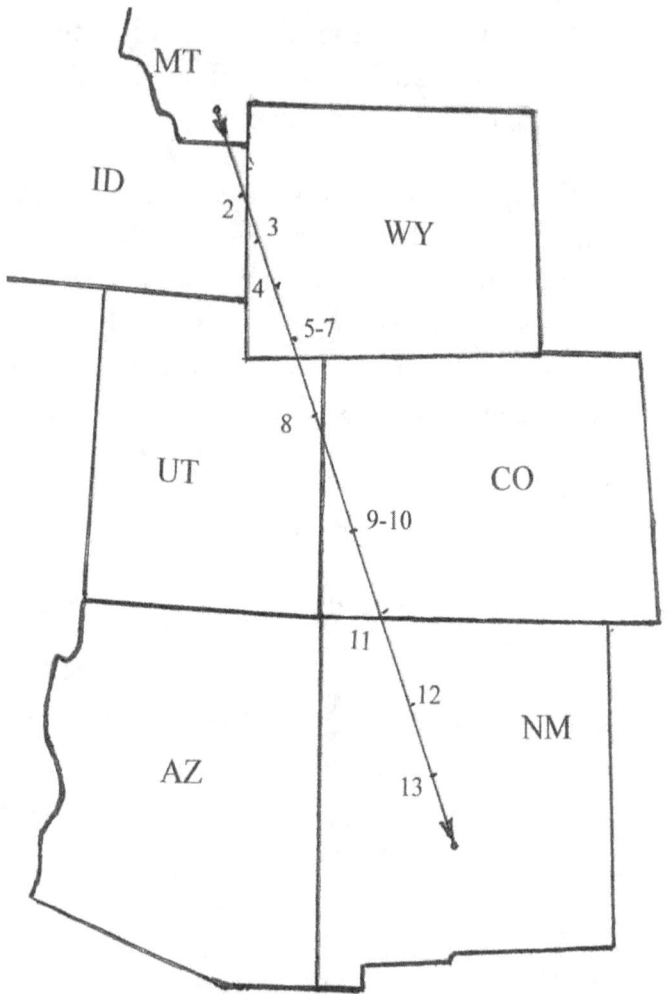

Figure 10. The Team's migration route from Montana to New Mexico with numbers indicating the starting points for Day Two through Day Thirteen.

CHAPTER 17

OUR WINTER HOME

Day Thirteen dawned picture-perfect. Team and mankind seemed eager and ready to fly. My friends were anxious to see what our winter home was like. I thought it must be pretty nice because so many cranes, geese, and ducks stayed there. Of course, we had never lived around so many other birds. I supposed we would have to get used to all the noise. Perhaps we would have to fight for a share of the food.

Alex and Hank seemed to be waiting for something before we could leave. Finally, several cars arrived and mankind got out carrying pieces of equipment. Someone said they were going to take pictures of us as we took off on the final flight of this history-making migration. Soon we were ready. Alex gave the signal and we took off. In the air we circled twice for the benefit of those taking pictures. Then Alex led us south-southeast.

Earlier Alex had said we would be following a river called the Rio Grande. When we reached it I was surprised. It was much different than the deep blue color of swift streams back home. It was much larger, brown, and seemed to flow slowly. I wondered if any fish could live in such muddy water. I also was interested in the countryside we flew over since we were close to our new home. In places the river was bordered by pasture and fields. Elsewhere there was thick brush, trees, and even old windblown sandy areas. The ground looked dry on low mesas farther from the river. Some were used as pasture for a few tough-looking cows. Short bushes were scattered about as though they were looking for water.

The day was warm, the sky blue with white cloud trails someone said were made by planes so high they looked like dragon flies. Time passed quickly. Team was healthy, strong, and looked sharp. Our chitchat was light with excitement and joking.

"Wow, I feel like we will soon be to the Promised Land, the place the Spirit told Firstborn we would reach through migration," said Ahiram. "I'm ready to just hang out there all winter."

"I also look forward to just staying in one place awhile and letting my wings have a vacation," responded Gad.

"Do you suppose the foods will be the same there or will they be different than those in Montana?" asked Deborah.

"I hope they are a mixture of the old and new, what we had in Montana and some new and exciting tastes at the refuge," answered Lois.

"I want it to be a place without golden eagles or coyotes. And I hope the mankind will chase off anything that would like to eat us," said Dorcas.

"Ono, do you remember that on the first day of migration I said you fly like an old goose. I must confess that during the entire trip you flew like a champion," said Gad.

"Why thank you Gad. I take back the bad things I said about your ability to fly, at least most of them," laughed Ono.

"I hate to admit that on our first flight I said Nimrod looked like a hummingbird on permanent overdrive," said Lois. "Perhaps a hungry buzzard would have been a better description of some of his circling to gain altitude," she chuckled.

"Well thanks a lot," Nimrod replied with pretended anger. "I love you too," he said. It appeared like he appreciated the attention she gave him.

The last hop in migration took about two hours. We must have been in view of mankind when there was a sudden burst of excited radio talk between Alex, Carl, and those awaiting us. Soon I could see trucks and cars parked behind a row of trees. Beneath the trees were groups of people pointing in our direction. They were looking through those two-eyed things called 'binoculars'.

"Phil, I'll make one pass southward directly over the people, then return and circle over the field so they get a good view and photos," Alex said, talking on the plane's radio with the refuge manager. "When we land, keep the people back by the tree line. I don't want them moving close where they might distract the birds,"

"Look sharp, Team," I instructed. "We will circle a little so the mankind below can get a good view of us."

We passed directly over the people, like Alex said, then made a gentle turn and passed over again. We were near the Rio Grande. I could see marshes and ponds in several directions. Clouds of snow geese rose up in the distance, disturbed by our planes. It was beautiful, like a snow blizzard. Sandhill cranes were flying in small groups. Hundreds were feeding in a field nearby. Bald eagles were sitting in trees along the river. Deer looked up at our plane as though curious, and not frightened.

I saw a flock of wild turkeys for the first time. How did I know they were called turkeys? It was that sudden inner knowing. It seemed to be one of the gifts promised by The Spirit of Living Creatures. Alfalfa and corn seemed to be the main thing growing in fields. The river was bordered with cottonwood trees and brush. Water flowed from the river into ditches and from there to ponds and marshes I could see in the distance. The water was tan, not blue as I had hoped, but showed promise of containing food.

Big Bird circled twice over an alfalfa field, losing altitude, and then landed gently. Some of us came down softly using strong wing downbeats to slow our descent. Others, in their excitement, wanted to show off, dipping back and forth with cupped wings. Their display drew a burst of noise from the watching mankind, some striking their hands together. Others said "ooh" or "ahh." It sounded like they were happy to see us.

At first I mainly watched the mankind. The ground crew approached the planes. Noticing we were thirsty from the flying and excitement, the mankind set out water containers. After drinking, I gave full attention to eating an alfalfa salad, sprinkled with lady bugs, leaf hoppers, and other special treats. People along the tree line began leaving. The sound of their trucks and cars faded in the distance.

Then I heard Alex calling us to follow. He was some distance away along the edge of a field of corn. My friends seemed eager to see whatever Alex wanted to show us in our winter home. Some flew a few feet above the ground in order to quickly reach him. The rest of us walked rapidly across the field, watching for further snacks along the way. As I approached, he continued to call softly. Alex walked bent over within the tall cornstalks as if hiding from something. We were led to the edge of the field where I had seen hundreds of sandhill cranes before we landed.

The wild cranes were feeding where corn stalks were flat on the ground. I thought the corn seeds must be good because the wild cranes eagerly ate them. Team members did not hesitate to move toward the wild cranes and the opportunity to try a new food item. Alex remained hidden in the field of standing corn.

Several pair of adult sandhill cranes showed particular interest in our Team and came towards us. They invited Izehar, and the other young sandhill cranes that migrated with us, to join them. Our friends, hungry for attention from adults of their own kind, answered their calls, but stayed with us.

However, after spending a few days on the refuge, we rarely saw Izehar and his buddies. Our sandhill companions were attracted to their own kind. They seemed to have been adopted by adult pairs of wild cranes. Although I missed these friends, I understood their desire to be with adults of their own kind. I missed my natural parents and would have joined adult whooping cranes if they had been present. Our sandhill companions had fulfilled their purpose of making us fairly comfortable around their species. As a result, we were able to learn, from the wild cranes, how to survive in our winter home.

Because sandhill cranes had been our companions since flight training, we were not afraid to approach the wild sandhill cranes. However, our little flock of youngsters still felt uncomfortable around their large flocks. So, we approached carefully. I felt uneasy, even though I was as tall as the adult male cranes.

"Mind if we join you?" I asked. The sandhills looked unfriendly and did not answer. Perhaps they did not know we also were cranes?

Raham was nearby. I tried a few grains of corn and considered the taste.

"Ah, it's like a rather bold protein sprinkled with a bit of hops."

"My impression exactly," she chortled.

We continued feeding. Raham moved farther to my right. Within minutes I heard her make a Guard Call, a high-pitched sound signifying fear or readiness to fight. A large male sandhill crane attempted to strike her head with his bill. She dodged the blow. I lost all caution when I saw him attacking her. Filled with anger, my neck extended forward, wings spread and drooped, I hissed and growled, signaling that I intended to attack.

The sandhill ignored my threat. "What do you want, Whitey?" referring sarcastically to my white feathers.

That only increased my angry response. With a leap forward, wings outspread, I was within range. I suppose he hadn't expected such a swift reaction. My longer neck was a definite advantage. He tried to dodge.

My beak, powered by muscles strong from probing in the ground, forcefully struck the top of his head. He staggered from the blow. Before he could recover, my second stab drew blood, catching him behind the bill. The third blow hit his left side above the wing, finishing the fight. He retreated across the field faster than I could move forward to thrash him with my wings. The fight attracted the attention of other wild cranes nearby.

"We have as much right to this food as you do. And we will enjoy it," I said firmly so all could hear me, still angry at the male's attack on Raham.

The sandhills seemed to decide not to mess with us and continued feeding. Those nearby slightly bowed their head and bodies, showing they recognized my authority.

"Are you okay, Raham?"

"Yes, I'm fine. Thank you," she said rather breathlessly. "That was certainly fast action. I don't believe I've ever seen you so angry, Firstborn."

"Oh, it angered me he wouldn't share food when there is so much here." My reaction surprised me. I seemed to have feelings for Raham I did not understand. I pretended my anger was about sharing kernels of corn. I was not ready to admit it was his attack on her that angered me.

I also realized I could not let the wild cranes bully me or my friends. It was the first of a number of such fights I and others had that winter. The sandhills obviously recognized us as being different. The adult females and juveniles, being smaller, did not attempt to bully us. Adult males seemed to enjoy attacking the female or smaller male members of our Team. Any whooping crane by itself was likely to become the target of several sandhill cranes. We learned to stay together much of the time to avoid fights. Or, we chose to feed outside the edge of large flocks of sandhills.

Despite the fight, I was already enjoying our winter home and appreciated our Creator, and Alex, for leading us there. That thought prompted me to look around. I was unable to see Alex. He led us to this field while staying hidden in standing corn. Perhaps he did not want to frighten the wild sandhill cranes. By leading us, he introduced us to plentiful food and to the wild sandhills. There was much more we would learn from these wild cranes in the following days and weeks. I learned to be thankful for how their alert, wary behavior helped protect our Team from dangers unfamiliar to us.

In the afternoon we learned a trick to use when feeding where cornstalks had been knocked down. Some ears of corn, covered with their dried leaves, were still attached to stalks. Sandhills would pick at the leaves with their bill to uncover the yellow kernels. We imitated their behavior, and ate our fill by picking kernels off the ear.

We continued resting, preening, and feeding. I was thirsty so I walked back to where we landed. I expected to find a water bowl, but the trucks and mankind were gone. Only the planes remained. The sun was steadily lowering so I rejoined my friends to finish my evening meal. Then we learned another valuable lesson about our winter home.

Coyotes were abundant. They loved to dine on any careless duck, goose, or crane. We were feeding on the edge of a flock of sandhill cranes as they fed among the flattened cornstalks. A young sandhill, feeding near some upright cornstalks, gave a distress call. A coyote, previously hidden in the standing corn, had him by the neck. He dragged the youngster, struggling and still calling, into the standing corn. Nearby cranes flew in fright; those farther away remained alert and walked away. Soon the distress calls stopped. The struggle was over. That frightening scene, easily remembered, definitely helped me to be cautious then, and in the future. It was too dangerous for birds to feed close to, or in standing corn, where a coyote or bobcat could hide.

Later, I saw how mankind set the dinner table for us birds. A man drove a tractor with a metal bar across the front and knocked down cornstalks. The tractor pulled something large, round, close to the ground, making a whirring, chopping sound. Cornstalks were knocked flat, or cut off, so we could walk among them. Sometimes ears of corn were knocked off the stalk and split open. It was easy feeding there. Every day the mankind knocked down a few more rows of corn so we had fresh food without entering the standing corn.

The sun dropped below the horizon. Small flocks of sandhills were taking flight, some heading south or southwest. Most were flying east, a little above treetop level. I suspected they were going to roost on the Rio Grande. I could hear hundreds of cranes calling from the direction of the river. I wondered when Alex would return to care for us and place us in our pen. Finally, the few remaining wild sandhills left and headed for their roost.

"Let's return to where the planes landed. Perhaps Alex is waiting there," I said.

CHAPTER 18

RIVER ROOST

That's when Alex arrived. He called us to follow. Walking across several fields, we approached woods along the Rio Grande. When Alex began running we flew slightly above him until he entered the woods. Then, as we flew above the treetops, I could still see him running toward the river's edge. A large sandbar, in the middle of the river, contained hundreds of sandhill cranes standing along the shoreline or in bordering shallow water. It seemed that Alex had led us to a place where we should roost.

We landed along one edge of the sandbar. I tried to see Alex along the wooded border of the river, but could not. He was not calling us. It seemed we were to spend the night there with the wild sandhill cranes. After satisfying my thirst, I bathed for the first time in many days. It felt great.

As nightfall deepened I moved off the sandbar to spend the night standing in shallow water. This water was much warmer than in mountain streams visited during our migration. The current flow against my legs had a soothing effect. Despite the noise, caused by so many cranes talking at once, I knew I would sleep well. I was tired from the exercise and exciting events of the day. I had been introduced to a new home, new food, new dangers, and an unfriendly sandhill crane. It had been a full day.

I was drifting off to sleep when I heard Raham's startled cry. Instantly alert, I looked about. I was unable to see any danger. She was roosting with Philetus and other friends farther down the shoreline. I began moving towards her. Philetus gave a distress call, leaped up, and flew to the sandbar. Raham repeated her distress call as I reached her side.

"What's wrong?"

"Something is rubbing against my leg!" she replied, shuddering.

"I don't see anything."

"Ohhhhhhh, there it is again!" She seemed frozen in fear.

Then something brushed against my right leg. In an automatic response I struck downward into something soft, yielding. It twisted upward, partially clearing the water surface. In light cast by the rising moon I saw the problem.

"It's only a carp," I said.

"Only!, - only!, - I think they are horrid. I don't like anything sneaking up on me and rubbing my legs at night. Would you?"

"It depends what it is," I answered. "Peck them. They will leave like that one did. They won't hurt you. I'd eat them, but they are too big."

"Oh, you would eat anything. You are - are - cold-hearted. How do you expect me to sleep here with these things rooting around in the mud?" Raham complained.

"How do you expect me to sleep with you screaming about a little carp?" I asked.

"Little! It was huge, ugly, scaly, and slippery," she replied with emphasis.

So she and her girlfriends were complaining about standing in water where fish might rub their legs. Females! There is no understanding them. I only tried to help her. Then she blames me for these fish. How ridiculous! I moved a greater distance away so I wouldn't have to hear their complaining. Soon I fell into a deep sleep on my first night at our winter home.

Dawn came gently. I enjoyed the last minutes of sleep. Sandhill cranes began leaving our sandbar, flying west in small groups. I drank deeply from the river, and then searched the shallows for minnows. No such luck. I saw Raham at a distance, but ignored her. No point repeating the argument of last night.

The bare sandbar offered no food. Back in the shallows I saw a slight movement indicating something alive. One quick strike, then a medium-sized crayfish became breakfast.

Soon, our Team and only a few dozen sandhill cranes remained on the sandbar. Then I heard Alex calling us from somewhere in woods bordering the river. Making flight-intention calls, we and a dozen wild sandhills took off and passed over the woods. I could not see Alex, but supposed he had gone towards the field where a large flock of cranes was again feeding in the corn. As we flew over the field where we arrived the previous day, I noticed the planes were gone. We settled near the wild cranes and began feeding, watching for Alex.

By late morning, sandhill cranes began flying to the river. Our Team soon had the cornfield to ourselves, but dry corn kernels and grasshoppers provided little moisture. The warm, early November day left me thirsty. I missed the water normally offered at midday following our morning flight. I walked along the field to a ditch that contained flowing water. After drinking, I led my friends to the ditch. The entire Team was able to drink, taking turns while some watched for danger.

A bald eagle approached, but showed no interest in us. We returned to the cornfield. By midafternoon the wild sandhill cranes returned from the river. They seemed refreshed by their river visit, ready for more corn. That afternoon was like the previous one except no coyote appeared. We heard Alex calling after most of the wild cranes had gone to roost. Again he led us to the river where we landed on the sandbar roost. In the evening we experienced another teaching for our class on "Introduction to Survival in the Wild."

Late at night I was awakened by alarm calls of sandhill cranes. A large flock soon took flight and headed downriver. I tried to see what disturbed them. Nothing seemed to be in the air except cranes. I was unable to see anything dangerous in trees bordering the river. Finally I saw the problem. Their heads were barely visible in the water. Moonlight glistened on the water disturbed behind their swimming bodies. Three coyotes were approaching our sandbar.

I gave an alarm call and led our Team downriver following the sandhills. The sky was clear. Moon and stars provided enough light so we could dodge branches of trees bordering the river. Following a wide ribbon of water, I passed over several sandbars crowded with cranes. Finally I saw a sandbar not fully occupied by cranes. We landed and remained until dawn.

Then I understood why the cranes roosted around sandbars in the center of the river. Coyotes could easily attack cranes roosting in shallow water along wooded borders of the river. In large crane flocks, some are awake and alert at all times of night. Most likely, some would see coyotes as they attempted to swim out to a sandbar, and warn the others, just as had happened that night.

At daybreak, sandhill cranes began leaving the roost, heading upriver. Soon, only our Team remained as we waited for Alex's call, but heard nothing. Perhaps Alex did not know where we were. Finally, I decided the Team should leave the sandbar. I led them upriver to the field where we fed the previous two days. I was certain Alex could find us there.

The sandhills had departed to the river for their midday rest when he appeared at a distance. He was in the edge of standing corn, watching us through binoculars. When he seemed confident we were the only cranes remaining in the field, he walked towards us. We were happy to see him. He was the one mankind our Team did not hesitate to approach. Perhaps he would be bringing us water or some food pellets. Pellets, like those I became tired of eating during migration, now seemed appealing.

We gathered near him. At first he was quiet and seemed to be studying each of us with great care as though drinking in memories of how we looked.

"Team, I'm so proud of you. I have not had a chance to tell you what a great job you did during migration and our arrival here. We went through a lot together and grew stronger as a result. I wish Nathan, Pasach, Spook, and Ragau were here to share our success."

Sensing his serious emotions, Team watched him intently, even though they did not understand his words. He paused as though remembering the tragic deaths of our friends, his eyes glistening.

"You seem to be adjusting well to your winter home. Now you must prove you can survive in the wild without man's help. It is time for me to return to the ranch and my family. Refuge workers will be watching you and telling me about your progress. I'll visit you in a few weeks."

I told the Team, "Alex said he is proud of us. We did a great job migrating here. We shared much danger. Now we are stronger and wiser. He wishes that our friends who died could have shared in our successful arrival. Now we need to prove we can survive here on the refuge without the help of mankind. He said it was time for him to return to the ranch." It was a serious moment as I thought about my friendship with Alex. I felt as though we were being abandoned.

Again he carefully looked at each of us. His love and appreciation were sensed, not spoken. "Learn from wild sandhills how to survive. Now you should join them at the river."

He turned as if to lead us to the river, paused, then turned to face me. "Firstborn, continue to lead them, buddy. Good luck."

He seemed to know the Team viewed me as their leader. Turning slowly, as if he hated to leave, he called us to follow one last time. With a determined look on his face, he began running. We gave flight-intention calls and lunged into the air. Flying slowly, slightly above Alex, calling repeatedly, we paraded towards the river.

I sensed it was an important moment without fully understanding what was happening. I had no idea how it would affect my future. Our calling celebrated this mankind who once was Mom, and later became our

Coach. We called our thanks for this one who expressed love to us. When he entered the trees bordering the Rio Grande, we continued our calling salute, gliding to a landing on the sandbar.

I did not realize, never again would I see him up close. He was cutting our tie with mankind. His desire was that we learn to survive in the wild. He wanted to prove that whooping cranes, raised in captivity, could be taught to migrate and start a new wild population. The same separation was true of Hank, Carl, and members of the chase crew. No longer would they be a part of our daily life.

Occasionally, through winter, I saw one or more mankind watching us. Perhaps it was Alex, Hank, or refuge workers. They knew we must learn to fear all mankind in order to survive. Whenever members of our Team became careless, and approached too close to humans, someone fired shotshells in our direction. These experiences taught us to stay away from humankind. Soon I learned more about why they could be dangerous.

CHAPTER 19

MANKIND ACCUSED

Leaves had been falling from cottonwood trees for several weeks when the first snowfall came. It started shortly before dawn, lasting only long enough to leave a white dusting on cornstalks. Several more weeks passed before winter arrived in full force. Snow and hard winds hit one midafternoon while we were feeding in a cornfield. Soon it was snowing so hard it became difficult to see more than twenty wingspans. Fortunately, the Team was together that afternoon.

"Let's move towards the middle of the field. I have an uneasy feeling," I told them. "I don't feel safe when I am unable to see very far." Later, the sense of danger proved true when a coyote, near the field's edge, captured a snow goose before it could take flight.

During a brief break in the storm, I decided we should fly to the roost earlier than usual. It also proved to be a wise choice. One flock of sandhill cranes stayed in the field until sunset. By then, in blizzard conditions, they had difficulty seeing and flying to the river. Several were killed when they hit a line between poles.

Several days later I was preening after feeding in a cornfield. A mallard drake walked by, limping. Two of his outer wing feathers were partially broken and hanging loose. My first thought was that he hit one of those lines strung between poles.

"What happened to you?" I asked.

"I had a close call when I was migrating from up north," answered the mallard. "Along the way my flock was about to land where other ducks were resting on a pond. Then I noticed the ducks on the water were not the real thing. Before I could escape, a mankind threw stuff at me, clipping my foot and these wing feathers. Two of my friends were killed."

"What do you mean the ducks were not the real thing?"

"The mankind made something to look like ducks and set them on the water to fool us," the mallard replied. "Then they imitated sounds like friendly ducks inviting us to land there. When we came close they pointed long sticks at us that made loud noises and threw little stones that could kill or injure us."

His answer surprised me. "Why do people do that?" I asked.

"I suppose they don't like us. Maybe they eat us like coyotes do. I don't know for sure. My grandfather and father warned me about them. I was careless. My foot is healing, and new feathers will grow out. I'll be wiser next time."

"I didn't realize some men could be so dangerous," I replied.

"Most of them are. Some feed us in parks, but don't let that fool you. You shouldn't trust any of them," the mallard said.

"The humans around here seem nice. They stand and watch us from a distance."

"This is a refuge, a place where animals are safe and protected," said the mallard. "When you leave here, you have to be cautious. Some mankind may point their sticks at you."

"Really! Why would they do that? My flock never felt threated by mankind," I replied. "We migrated a long ways. It took us many days. We were never harmed. We saw mankind all along the way."

"You were lucky. Up north I saw a mankind carrying two dead sandhill cranes across a field," said mallard. "I imagine they might eat you guys too. Be careful when you leave the refuge. It seems like they only throw those stones at us in fall and winter. Watch your back." The mallard limped away between rows of downed corn.

It was upsetting to think some mankind might try to kill us. It made no sense. We are an endangered species. People are trying to keep us from becoming extinct. Alex and his friends fed and protected us. Humans visited us during our migration stops and seemed friendly. Of course there was one man who asked if we were good to eat. However, he was the exception.

Maybe men do not like mallard ducks for some reason. Perhaps mallards eat mankind's food or harm them in some other way. Certainly there must be a good reason for what happened. Surely we cranes had nothing to fear.

But I was unable to convince myself that mallard was wrong. He seemed honest and concerned about me. Then I remembered. One of the reasons whooping cranes are endangered is because mankind hunted our forefathers for meat. However, that was many years ago. Since then we have been protected. It was a confusing matter. Some men were protecting us, and trying to increase our populations. Yet others might try to hurt us. I would have to stay alert, to watch my back, like mallard said, and my front!

I soon became used to the daily routine. We flew from the river roost at daybreak to feed in corn or alfalfa fields. At midday we returned to drink and rest by Rio Grande sandbars. By midafternoon it was again time to fly to feeding fields. At dusk we returned to the river. After I had been on the refuge for a few weeks, I was feeling comfortable in this newfound freedom. We were not shut in a pen at night. We could eat our fill during the day without waiting for Alex to bring pellets.

Not many days later we received the first clue that Alex had returned to see how we were doing. At midafternoon we flew from the Rio Grande expecting to feed in a cornfield where we had been that morning.

As we approached in the air, Gad said, "Look, Firstborn. One of our Team is already in the field."

Sure enough, it was one of our species. I was surprised. I thought we had been the first of our flock to leave the river for the afternoon feeding.

"Hello," called Ono.

"Hello," was the response.

"Why it looks like Midian. Are my eyes fooling me?" asked Ono.

"If they are, my eyes are doing the same," I said.

We sailed to a gentle landing beside him. "Midian, how are you? How did you get here?" asked Gad.

"Hey, Firstborn! Gad! Ono! It's good to see old friends again. Mom -- uh, I mean Alex -- brought me here in a truck," said Midian. "A little while ago he released me in this field."

"Wow, you are looking good. Welcome to our winter home," I said, but I felt uncomfortable around this companion who left, perhaps deserted us, at the beginning of the migration. Still, I wanted to be polite.

Ono asked, "Alex brought you here?"

"Yes, I became separated from the flock that first day of migration. While escaping from an eagle I lost my way and could not find the Team. So then I flew back to the ranch. A mankind let me back in our home pen and fed me. I was still there when Alex returned to the ranch. Yesterday he placed me in a truck and brought me here. I was pretty scared when he drove off and left me alone."

"We returned here after loafing on a sandbar in the Rio Grande. We have been feeding in this field for several days. The rest of the Team will be here soon. It is good to see you again," I said. "Evidently Alex knew we would be coming to feed here where you could join us."

I did not see Alex, although I eagerly watched for him. I was sure he was somewhere out there watching us from a distance. I suppose he wanted Midian to join us, to learn how to survive in the wild.

The others soon returned from the river and greeted Midian. In the days that followed, his closer friends told him about our adventures during migration. He seemed to envy all we had experienced.

I remembered that Alex told me to continue leading the Team. So, I told Midian how to avoid danger and where to find food. I wanted to be helpful. But my feelings toward him were nothing like the close friendships I had with those who faced danger with me as we migrated.

We had shared grief at the death of friends. Midian had not shared those experiences. I think he saw himself as an outsider. Maybe he felt guilty about not finding us after being separated the first morning we migrated. Anyway, he mostly followed behind our Team or spent time alone.

A few days later the Team was returning to the sandbar roost for the evening. Midian saw two sandhill cranes feeding on minnows in shallows bordering the riverbank.

"Achor, I'm hungry for some fresh fish. Let's land near those sandhills and catch a few minnows," said Midian.

"I'm not hungry. I'm full of corn and more interested in relaxing on the sandbar," Achor replied.

"Okay, I'll join you there after I down a few." Midian turned and started to glide towards the pair of sandhills.

*****

After dark, Abagtha walked over to me.

"Firstborn, I was talking with Achor a moment ago. Midian did not return to the sandbar. But, earlier he told Achor he would join us here in a little while. He stopped along the river edge to catch a few minnows where he saw a pair of sandhill cranes fishing. I'm worried about him. He is not wise to all the dangers around here."

"Perhaps he decided to roost with the sandhill cranes. I imagine he will join us in the morning," I answered. "I don't think you need to worry about him."

My words did not seem to reassure Abagtha. Sometimes females have a sixth sense about trouble. I also did not feel comfortable about his absence. But we could not go looking for him in the dark.

Leaving the roost the next morning we flew over the area where Midian planned to fish for minnows. No birds were present. When he still failed to appear later in the day, some of us discussed the matter.

"I believe I recognized one of the sandhill cranes fishing along the river where Midian landed last evening. I'll keep an eye out for him. When I find him, I'll see if he knows where Midian might be," said Achor.

The inquiry by Achor became unnecessary when a sandhill crane approached Ono that afternoon.

"Excuse me, but is one of your friends missing?" the sandhill said.

"Yes, one named Midian was last seen yesterday evening. He was going to feed on minnows along the Rio Grande. Why do you ask?"

"I thought I should tell someone in your flock what happened last evening," said the sandhill. "A friend and I were feeding on minnows along the river edge. It may have been your friend who landed near us.

"He stayed at a distance, closer to the shoreline. Perhaps he did not want to disturb us or to appear to be interfering with our fishing. I think he caught a few minnows. We were busy getting a few more before flying to roost. I heard a big splash, looked around, and saw him struggling in shallow water.

"A bobcat had jumped from brush along the riverbank. It was biting the crane's lower neck, gripping the upper body with its front paws. I'm sorry. As I took flight, the crane was thrashing the cat with its wings. As we circled, I looked below. The bobcat was dragging your friend, no longer struggling, up the bank."

Sadly, the sandhill crane's tale was enough to solve the mystery of what happened to Midian. I felt bad. Another of our original group was gone. Somehow I felt partly to blame for Midian's death. Perhaps I had not done enough to help him learn how to survive in the wild.

It seemed like there were new things to learn and teach the others every day. Sometimes the lessons came quickly, forced upon us. The next one was also very hard to accept.

CHAPTER 20

AN ENEMY REVEALED

As time passed, our Team was less frequently together as a group. They, like me, were learning more about this exciting new life. Two, three, or more members were exploring other feeding fields and roosting sites, or spending time feeding near flocks of sandhill cranes or geese.

Sometimes I chose to roost with my closest friends in ponds or marshes in other parts of the refuge. Unlike the bare sandbars of the Rio Grande, these ponds offered other abundant foods like plant tubers, crayfish, frogs, minnows, and greens. Because our legs were long, we could stand in shallow water at some distance from the shoreline. That distance from the shoreline gave us the opportunity to take flight and escape from anything that might try to rush out and grab us. The splashing noise, as any coyote or bobcat ran through the water, would alert us to danger.

Throughout the night, these ponds were noisier than river roosts used only by cranes. Blackbirds, ducks of many kinds, snow geese, Canada geese, cranes, herons, frogs, yes, and sometimes even coyotes and raccoons, added to a nighttime chorus. You might think it would be difficult to sleep. Except for the dangerous sounds, it was music to my ears. Some birds were awake at any time during the night. Many alert eyes and ears added to our safety. Sometimes our alarm clock was silence, signaling a coyote, fox, or bobcat was nearby, watched by many eyes.

After such a night, Ono, Gad, and I flew north at midmorning to join others of our group at a cornfield where we often fed. We usually saw all the other Team members sometime during a day to catch up on the latest news. As we approached, I could easily recognize our group by their size and white coloration. After landing, I greeted them. "Good morning, how is everyone?"

Raham rushed over. "Oh, Firstborn, I'm so happy you are okay! I was worried something bad might have happened to you also."

"What do you mean, also?" I asked.

"Haven't you heard about Maath and Lois? The mankind killed them!" She replied angrily. "They fell, crashing to the ground."

"What! - how do you know that is true?"

"Mibzar told us. He's over there," Raham said, pointing with her bill.

I looked in the direction she motioned. Mibzar was resting on the ground looking sad. Followed by my shocked companions, I walked over to where he rested. Feeling a mixture of anger, disbelief, and tenderness, I asked, "Mibzar, what happened?"

Mibzar did not stand, raised his head slowly, fixing his sad eyes on mine. "Oh, Firstborn, we were talking with some sandhill cranes at the river roost last night. They told us about a field they visited last winter outside of the refuge. The mankind had grown something called peanuts and harvested what they could. There were still lots of delicious peanuts left for the sandhill cranes to eat when they visited the fields. So they wondered if peanuts might have been planted there this year or in other nearby fields. And they invited us to fly up north with them in the morning to see if they could find peanuts.

"After sunrise, Maath, Lois, and I joined seven sandhill cranes. Soon they recognized the field. One said, 'Look, there are already a few cranes there.'"

Mibzar continued, his voice trembling, "I saw the cranes. Some seemed alert with heads up. Others had their bills touching the ground as though feeding. They didn't seem to be moving. Still, I did not sense danger. We turned, cupped our wings, preparing to land." He paused – as if it was a struggle to continue speaking. –

"The sandhill cranes with us were making contact calls. Then I realized something was not right. The cranes in the field were not answering. By then I was close enough to see that those cranes did not look quite right."

Again Mibzar paused – then his voice became almost soprano-like. He spoke rapidly as though desiring to finish his story so he could stop remembering those terrible moments. "Something's wrong! I shouted. It was too late. Some mankind stood up from holes where they had hidden in the ground. They pointed dark sticks at us that made loud noises. Maath, Lois, and three sandhill cranes collapsed, twisting in the air, crashing to the ground. The rest of us were frantically trying to escape. We turned back towards the refuge. A sandhill crane, the one who told us about last year's peanuts, seemed hurt. He was unable to fly as fast as the rest of us.

"I slowed down and flew beside him." – Mibzar again paused, as though he had to catch his breath. – His speech slowed and returned to the tenor tone. "I spoke to the sandhill and said, I think we are over the refuge now and safe. Is there any way I can help you?"

"He looked at me with sad eyes, didn't answer, and went limp. - His body tumbled through the air, striking tree limbs before crumpling to the ground. Oh, Firstborn, I am so sad and angry!"

"I'm so sorry, so terribly sorry, and angry too. How could mankind do such a terrible thing to our friends?" I replied. I didn't know what else to say. I was too shocked to fully understand what had happened. I was unable to believe that my friends were gone. Together we had survived through so many difficulties.

Then I knew what the mallard said was true. I needed to tell our Team to stay on the refuge until spring. Then it might be safe for us to start the migration northward. We needed to stay on the refuge until it was safe to proceed north.

Storms swept across the area every few weeks during winter. Snow cover lasted only a few days or sometimes a week or more before it vanished during warm spells. Refuge workers continued to knock down rows of corn for our benefit. It was the only food easily found. At least it was enough so we did not lose weight. Ponds and marshes were sometimes covered with ice. Then we had to roost on sandbars kept free of ice by the river current.

Finally, judging by the battle between winter and spring, I could tell winter was losing. No longer did I hear those bangs, evidence mankind were still hunting outside the refuge. Like the mallard said, now it might be safe to fly outside the refuge.

I was restless, uneasy with new inner feelings that later built into the urge to migrate north. The activity of us whoopers, and the sandhill cranes, changed to include daily flights over the refuge. Sometimes, we flew several miles north before we returned. Wing and breast muscles had become lazy, making only short local flights since first arriving at the refuge. These needed to be strengthened.

Flights began about midmorning after sun warmed the air above fields. This air would rise up like a natural elevator. Then it was easier to lazily spiral upward with normal flap flying. Sometimes our circling ended at some moderate altitude before we headed north. On other occasions we spiraled farther up until, to anyone on the ground, we would have looked like specks against a background of high fluffy clouds. This flying strengthened our bodies for spring migration. The exercise also helped calm my eagerness to return north.

An experience on a sandbar roost was enough to make me sleep lighter the following nights. I awoke about daybreak to discover a pair of great horned owls on a sandbar nearby eating a sandhill crane. No one witnessed their attack or heard the victim cry out. Evidently they silenced the crane before it could make any noise. Tracks indicated the crane walked from the shallow water where it roosted. Upon reaching the sandbar's edge, an owl struck it.[11]

It was too early to migrate. It could be dangerous to leave too soon, before winter storms weakened. Winter had not yet fully released its grip on New Mexico.

---

[11] Great horned owls are night predators with special feathers that allow them to fly more quietly than other birds. Normally they do not attack prey as large as grown cranes. However, these owls occasionally kill adult sandhill cranes in early spring when they have hungry young to feed and other foods are scarce. The owls seem bolder, or more desperate, at that time of year.

Figure 11. Team members exercise in high altitude flights above the refuge before spring migration. Three whooping cranes are followed by sandhill cranes. Notice the black wing tips on the whooping cranes. These black feathers are not visible when the wing is folded against the body.

The first flock of sandhill cranes that migrated to Colorado returned two days later. They reported food was scarce because the ground was still covered with snow. Also the marshes were frozen and not safe places to roost.

Day length gradually increased and it seemed that spring had finally arrived. Large flocks of sandhill cranes began leaving headed for Monte Vista or Alamosa

National Wildlife refuges in southern Colorado. They planned to stay there several weeks before moving farther north. Our feeding fields and roost sites gradually became quieter. It was obvious that large numbers of cranes migrated because there were fewer birds on feeding fields and roost sites.

One warm spring morning, Mibzar and Abagtha said they planned to migrate soon with a flock of sandhills. "We are anxious to get started. We would like all of you to join us."

The invitation seemed directed at me as leader. "I'm not in a hurry to leave. I imagine conditions in Colorado are now okay for roosting and feeding. However, I plan to wait a little longer before migrating. You certainly have my best wishes for a safe trip. I expect to see you up north later this summer."

I thought others would join them, but no one did. So, we told them goodbye, and they left.

The large numbers of cranes, ducks, and geese on the refuge were rapidly becoming a thing of the past. Huge flocks of snow geese departed for their Arctic nesting grounds. Most of the ducks had migrated. Flocks of sandhill cranes were leaving daily. No longer was the corn buffet provided fresh each morning. All the corn fields had been knocked down to feed wildlife.

Farm fields being plowed for spring planting provided earthworms, grubs, and small nutlets from wild grasses that managed to grow between last year's corn rows.

Alfalfa fields offered tender young leaves and bugs. The warmer weather woke up insects and frogs to add to our diet.

Snowmelt in the northern mountains meant increased flow in the Rio Grande, flooding the river sandbars used for roosting. I switched to roosting in the marshes. It was a nice time to be on the refuge, but there were problems. For one thing, the same number of coyotes had fewer birds to hunt. For those of us who remained on the refuge that meant we were more likely to be a target for some coyote's dinner.

The numbers of our Team became fewer in the following weeks as they departed north in twos and threes. Finally, only five remained. One day the others told me they planned to migrate the next morning.

I had injured a wing muscle in the midwinter battle with coyote that I told you about earlier. I felt it needed to heal a little longer before I migrated. But I did not tell them about my wing. My friends were so eager to leave I did not want to delay them. They continued to urge me to join them, but without success.

"You go ahead. I'm not quite ready to leave. Soon I'll join you in Colorado."

"Firstborn, if you won't leave with us, I refuse to leave you here alone. I will stay until you are ready to leave," said Raham.

I was thankful for her offer because I did not want to be alone. Her offer satisfied the concern the others had about leaving me alone. They left the next morning after we promised to join them soon at Monte Vista National Wildlife Refuge in Colorado. Their departure opened a brand new experience in my life.

Figure 12. At five months of age, Raham and Firstborn are beginning to get their white adult plumage. Male whooping cranes are larger than females.

CHAPTER 21

HEADING HOME

The next few days were especially pleasant. The weather was what spring should be, warm with gentle breezes, flowers of varied colors, birds singing their nesting songs, new life bursting forth everywhere. I was free from the duties of Team leadership. We could feed and roost wherever and whenever we wished. Worshipping our Creator together was a special privilege. Sunrises and sunsets were brilliant as though made only for us.

The days seemed to fly by. My wing quickly finished healing. Soon it was time to join our friends in Colorado. Yet, I was not in a hurry. The months spent at Bosque del Apache National Wildlife Refuge had been good. Yet that was not the reason I was slow to leave. I simply did not want to end the special time alone with Raham.

There were wonderful things about her I had not noticed before. I wondered how I failed to see how beautiful she was. Her eyes sparkled so, and the gentle purr greeting when she first awoke. Her graceful walk, that special look when I spoke, made me wonder why I felt so happy around her.[12]

When we actually headed north from the refuge, I felt the timing was right. I was eager to accomplish the return flight to Montana. On the first evening, we stopped at a secluded part of Cochiti Lake north of Albuquerque. A pleasant marsh offered a variety of foods. We roosted in a cove where shallow waters extended quite a distance from the shore. The air was calm and sky cloudless. We talked about what we had seen in the day's flight.

When the last remnant of daylight faded from the west, we were amazed at the multitude of stars adorning the sky. They seemed especially brilliant just for our enjoyment. For a brief time we were quiet as we admired their beauty. The word "stars" seemed to bring a thought

---

[12] Whooping cranes begin to form pairs when they are two or three years old. Females first lay eggs at age three or four years. The female produces two eggs per year. In the wild, the parents take turns incubating the eggs. The eggs hatch after thirty to thirty-five days.

to my mind. "Raham, the mankind's Bible says 'The heavens declare the glory of God: ... There is no speech nor spoken word [from the stars]; their voice is not heard. Yet their voice [in evidence] goes out through all the earth, their sayings to the end of the world.'" (Psalm 19:1-4a). I thought about this truth as I drifted off to sleep.

Our flight to Colorado was a lazy one with stops at the slightest excuse to examine lake and river borders, or fields promising favored foods. Sandhill cranes fly from Bosque del Apache refuge to Monte Vista National Wildlife refuge in one day, or at the most two. It took us five days.

As we approached in late afternoon, the ponds at Monte Vista National Wildlife Refuge were visible at a great distance. Soon it was easy to see the white feathering of our friends. As our altitude diminished, in a slow glide we approached the field they occupied.

Their calls of greeting reached us. "Firstborn, Raham, we were becoming concerned. We thought you might rejoin us sooner. It is so good to see you again."

"And we are happy to see you. How is everyone? What news do you have?" Our reunion conversations, as we ate and shared about happenings and friends, lasted until roost time.

Seven of our Team had not yet flown on north to summering sites. It was a joy to catch up on the news, to hear about things they had experienced. We stayed at Monte Vista refuge only a few days. The weather was rapidly warming. Others in our Team wanted to visit places in Idaho and western Wyoming, areas that sandhill cranes told us about. I was eager to continue north to my goal, that familiar valley in southwestern Montana.

I could picture the river south of the ranch, bordered by marshy areas, rich with foods I had learned to enjoy. I wanted to feed once more in the irrigated fields where we played as chicks. The place where The Spirit of Living Creatures first spoke to me had a special attraction.

And I hoped to see Alex. I wanted him to know that I, like others in our group, safely migrated north. I felt it was important to return to the ranch, to complete the migration. It would prove the technique could be used to start new populations of whooping cranes. Raham also wanted to return to the ranch and visit the fields where we grew up. So, we did.

It was already getting dark when we finally arrived at the ranch several days after leaving southern Colorado. We roosted in the trout pond at the base of the mountain.

The next morning was clear and calm with a bright sun. After our long migration, I was lazy. I was in no hurry to leave the roost to feed. Eventually, thoughts about breakfast stimulated us to take a short flight into a field west of the pen where we were raised. Before we landed, I thought I saw someone moving in the distance outside the ranch house.

*****

Tiana, Alex and Grace's oldest daughter, ran to the door of the ranch house. "Daddy, two of the whooping cranes are back."

"Are you certain they are whoopers? Sandhill cranes can look white at a distance when the sun is reflecting off their grey feathers," replied Alex.

"They are quite white. I don't think it's caused by the sun's reflection. They landed in the upper field."

"It could be some of our birds. The last time I phoned the manager at Monte Vista National Wildlife Refuge he said all the whoopers had moved on north. I'll get the receiver and see if we can hear any signal from a transmitter."

In a few minutes, Alex returned and turned on the receiver, pointing the antenna toward the upper field. Adjusting the dials, he searched for any signal that would identify a crane that migrated the previous fall. He heard nothing.

"Sorry, Tiana, it must be a pair of wild sandhill cranes, those that often nest in the valley."

Tiana, while looking through the binoculars, spoke excitedly. "Wait, they took flight! They are in the air now. Their wingtips look black like whoopers. Try for a signal again. I know you can receive a transmitter's signal at a greater distance when birds are in the air."

Alex moved the receiver's dials, pointing the antenna toward the birds, listening for a signal. On the seventh selection, the signal was loud and clear. His face lit up with a wide grin. "By golly, it's Firstborn! It's the signal from Firstborn's transmitter. He's back. He got here before the others. He's first again.

*****

I turned to Raham, flying close on my right. "It looks like someone is behind the ranch house, looking in our direction. Let's swing over that way and see if it's Alex."

"That would be wonderful!" replied Raham. "I am not afraid to fly near Alex. I would love to see him once more, even if it's only as we fly over."

*****

"They are turning this way," said Grace.

"I'll call the others so they can see them," said Alex.

Alex ran to the house. "Children, come out and see the whooping cranes! Some have come home."

Figure 13. We roosted at the trout pond after the long migration and were slow about flying to a neighboring field for breakfast.

*****

"Raham, the larger one looks like Alex, the others may be his mate and young," I said.

"It does look like Alex. Oh, this is so exciting!" responded Raham.

*****

"Tiana, can I look with the binoculars?" asked Alex.

"Sure." Tiana handed him the binoculars.

"I wonder who that is with Firstborn?" said Alex softly as though speaking to himself.

Alex turned from looking through the binoculars, "Firstborn has put on weight and muscle, but I would know him anywhere. I believe the other bird is number 'Twenty-seven' who often flew close to him in migration. Here, Grace, take a look."

"Oh wouldn't it be wonderful if they settle in our valley for the summer," said Tiana.

"That would be great," replied Alex.

*****

Then I was close enough to see details of the family. "That's Alex. Raham, let's give him and his family the salute they deserve," I said.

And so we did, circling over the ranch house, calling a salute to the one who sacrificed, worked so hard, and risked his life to ensure our kind would survive as a species.

*****

The girls jumped up and down and the Wilson family waved in greeting. "Hello Firstborn! Hello Twenty-seven! Welcome home! Welcome home!"

EPILOGUE

TO YOU THE READER: You also are *ONE CHOSEN* uniquely formed in your mother's womb (Psalm 139:13-15). The Creator placed special spiritual and physical gifts within you. This is true even if you are not the first child born by your mother. These abilities will only fully develop when you become a partner with the One True God of the Universe. His plan for you is for good, an abundant life, to give you hope and a purpose. Unfortunately, some refuse that opportunity. Your age makes no difference. Everyone has the opportunity to accomplish good things for Him and for their companions here on Earth. If you choose to follow the good path, you will experience some individuals, like Midian, who oppose you and the Creator. There likely will be something like mountains in your pathway, or strong winds that try to blow you off course, things similar to eagles and bobcats to avoid, and especially some mankind who serve a false god and seek to defeat your purpose. If you keep your eyes and heart fixed on the Creator, and listen to His instructions, you will achieve His goals for you just like Firstborn did.   Jim

ABOUT THE AUTHOR

Jim's first professional positions included being a field biologist and Research Supervisor for the Tennessee Game and Fish Commission. Later, while employed by the U.S. Fish and Wildlife Service, he was an Associate Professor at Oklahoma State University, an Associate Professor at the University of Georgia, and an Endangered Species Biologist. He is author of *The World of the Wild Turkey* (Lippincott), chapters in six other books, and numerous other articles. He has received a dozen awards for his conservation work and was an invited speaker at International Conferences in the USSR, China, and South Africa. A church Elder for the past 14 years, he formerly was President of a Gideon's International Camp and has been an officer of the Whooping Crane Conservation Association since 2002.

www.ingramcontent.com/pod-product-compliance
Lightning Source LLC
Chambersburg PA
CBHW071342280526
45787CB00001B/184